Startup Journey Idea To Entrepreneurial Triumph

Startup Journey Idea To Entrepreneurial Triumph

Rafeal Mechlore

UNIEK ENTERPRISES

CONTENTS

INDEX

Chapter 5:Pivoting and Adapting
5.1. Recognizing the need for change
5.2. Making critical business decisions
5.3. Strategies for successful pivots
5.4. Learning from failure

Chapter 6:Scaling and Growth
6.1. Achieving profitability
6.2. Scaling the business operations
6.3. Gaining market share
6.4. Disrupting industries and creating impact

Chapter 7:The Role of Mentorship
7.1. The importance of guidance and support
7.2. The impact of experienced entrepreneurs
7.3. Navigating the entrepreneurial ecosystem
7.4. Building a valuable network

Introduction

In the unique scene of the advanced business world, new companies have arisen as the vanguards of development and financial development. They address the encapsulation of thoughts, dreams, and the faithful soul of business. A startup's process is an exhilarating, frequently wild, ride from the underlying flash of a plan to the zenith of pioneering achievement. It's a story set apart by dangers, challenges, and resolute assurance that rejuvenates thoughts and changes them into flourishing organizations.

The expression "startup" itself embodies a feeling of crude, unrestrained energy and a desire to rock the boat. These enterprising endeavors aren't just about bringing in cash; they're tied in with taking care of issues, disturbing business sectors, and making enduring effect. Their accounts, similar to those of Apple, Google, and Amazon, have turned into the stuff of legends, rousing endless people to leave on their own excursions of creation and development.

While the objective might be a flourishing business, the way from ideation to enterprising victory is full of vulnerabilities. The excursion starts with a straightforward yet influential thought, which might strike its maker out of the blue - while washing up, having some espresso, or during a restless evening. This underlying flash, in any case, is only a glimpse of something larger. It follows that changes a simple idea into an undeniable business, an excursion laden with fervor, challenges, and vast potential outcomes.

Transforming that crude thought into the truth is very difficult, and the beginning phases of a startup's life are frequently described by vulnerability and chance. Business people should wrestle with inquiries of plausibility, market interest, and rivalry. They should explore the mind boggling snare of strategies, financial backer pitches, and statistical surveying. These beginning stages can measure up to the most common way of turning harsh, whole precious stones into shining diamonds, requiring persistence and talented hands to shape them into something significant.

The idea of a startup is naturally connected with development. It is tied in with taking a creative thought and thinking for even a moment to transform it into a substantial answer for existing issues or neglected needs. This development, be it innovative, process-situated, or market-driven, is the soul of new businesses. It separates them from laid out ventures and permits them to disturb laid out businesses, making new market specialties.

Inventive reasoning and an innovative attitude are fundamental elements of this excursion. Business visionaries should consider some fresh possibilities, persistently adjust to changes, and be prepared to turn when fundamental. The capacity to see open doors in challenges and adjust quickly is many times the way to endurance and, at last, win.

Hazard and vulnerability are not simply aspect of the game; they are essential to it. The eagerness to confront vulnerability, and in some cases even hug it, is a principal quality of fruitful business visionaries. The startup venture is filled with obscure factors - market changes, contest, and unanticipated deterrents. Embracing hazard and transforming it into a determined bet is where the rush untruths.

While new businesses are driven by the quest for advancement and the excitement of the obscure, they likewise work in a climate of restricted assets. Subsidizing, or the scarcity in that department, is a consistent worry for business visionaries. New businesses are not just asset obliged; they are many times established on a tight financial plan. Searching for capital from individual reserve funds, credits, or the thoughtfulness of private supporters is important for the early excursion.

One could scrutinize the insight of beginning a business with such small means, however this asset shortage has an approach to rearing development. It powers business visionaries to be thrifty, productive, and imaginative in their methodology. They figure out how to accomplish more with less and focus on the main thing for the business' development.

In this mission for assets, pitching to financial backers turns into a soul changing experience for new businesses. The "brief presentation," a brief and convincing show, turns into an organizer's dearest companion in this undertaking. It is a represent the deciding moment second, where business visionaries should convince financial backers that their thought merits backing. The capacity to express a dream, exhibit market understanding, and venture areas of strength for an of responsibility is critical. This expertise frequently ends up being all around as indispensable as the actual development.

To outcasts, the startup excursion could appear to be a thrilling rollercoaster ride. Nonetheless, it's not all adrenaline and highs. The excursion is likewise set apart by innumerable evenings of uneasiness and self-question. Business visionaries should explore the profound rollercoaster that goes with the job - the anxiety toward disappointment, the strain to succeed, and the penances made on an individual level.

The capacity to drive forward despite affliction is one more principal attribute of effective business people. The startup venture is a trial of versatility. It requires a psychological determination to beat the inescapable misfortunes and frustrations. It's normal for business visionaries to encounter different disappointments prior to tracking down the triumphant recipe.

Systems administration, mentorship, and an emotionally supportive network can be important in assisting business people with enduring these hardships. The startup local area is a very close one, with a culture of sharing encounters, illustrations learned, and loaning some assistance. Mentorship, specifically, is a directing light for some business visionaries, offering intelligence, bits of knowledge, and a significant organization that can open entryways and offer imperative help.

The significance of mentorship is difficult to exaggerate, as it assists business people with keeping away from normal entanglements and advantage from the encounters of the individuals who have strolled the way before them. It can give a guide through the frequently confounding territory of business tasks and development methodologies.

Yet, it's not only the singular's excursion; it's the group's excursion as well. Building a firm and skilled group is a foundation of startup achievement. The business person might give the underlying vision, yet the group makes an interpretation of that vision right into it. Building the right group, one that has a similar energy and devotion, is a craftsmanship in itself. It requires distinguishing the qualities and shortcomings of colleagues, adjusting their objectives to the organization's central goal, and encouraging a culture of joint effort and development.

The startup venture is likewise set apart by the requirement for consistent variation. The business scene is steadily advancing, and new companies should be coordinated to get by. They should be ready to turn their plan of action, change their objective market, or adjust their item or administration to the evolving conditions.

Being too unbending or resolute is a recipe for disappointment. Business visionaries should figure out how to peruse the market and change their sails as needs be. This capacity to adjust and turn is in many cases the life saver that keeps new companies above water during fierce times.

It's not only the outer climate that new companies should explore; they should likewise oversee interior difficulties. As a startup develops, the intricacies increment. Scaling a business brings its own arrangement of difficulties, from recruiting and preparing representatives to overseeing income and functional proficiency. This progress from a little, deft startup to a more organized association requires cautious preparation and execution.

Promoting and marking are additionally significant parts of the startup venture. A convincing item or administration should be promoted successfully to arrive at its interest group. New companies should recognize their remarkable incentive and make a brand that reverberates with their clients. Building areas of strength for a presence and utilizing computerized promoting procedures are many times fundamental to startup outcome in the present advanced age.

Lawful and administrative difficulties can add further intricacy. New companies should explore the multifaceted snare of licensed innovation security, agreements, and consistence with different regulations and guidelines. Dismissing lawful viewpoints can bring about exorbitant difficulties or even the downfall of the business.

One of the achievements of the startup venture is getting the main client. This second addresses approval of the thought and a critical stage towards supportability. The excitement of handling that first arrangement can be a defining moment in the existence of a startup, and it frequently denotes the change from endurance mode to development mode.

Scaling and development accompany their own arrangement of difficulties. New companies should consider issues like production network the board, planned operations, and extending their client base. The strain to satisfy developing need while keeping up with quality and consumer loyalty can overpower.

Much of the time, accomplishing benefit is a long and difficult interaction. New businesses frequently work in the red for a really long time, reinvesting income into development and extension. This requires discipline and key monetary administration to guarantee that the business stays practical.

A definitive objective of numerous new companies is to accomplish a leave procedure. Whether through securing by a bigger organization or opening up to the world through a first sale of stock (Initial public offering), an exit addresses the perfection of long stretches of difficult work and a huge monetary prize for the pioneers and financial backers. In any case, even the exit isn't the finish of the excursion yet a fresh start, as it presents new difficulties and open doors.

In the cutting edge startup scene, innovation assumes a huge part. The computerized age has democratized business, making it more straightforward for people and little groups to create and send off items and administrations that can contact a worldwide crowd. Innovation speeds up development, empowers remote work, and gives instruments to cooperation and it were beforehand impossible to scale that.

The crossing point of innovation and business venture has led to another type of new companies known as "tech new businesses." These organizations are frequently at the front line of development, utilizing state of the art innovation to disturb existing enterprises. They are portrayed by quick development, enormous scope subsidizing adjusts, and a worldwide reach.

Tech new businesses have their own extraordinary difficulties and open doors. They frequently face extraordinary contest, from laid out players as well as from different new companies with comparative thoughts. The requirement for specialized ability, licensed innovation insurance, and network protection is central. Nonetheless, the potential for monstrous achievement and worldwide effect is likewise critical.

As of late, the startup venture has advanced in light of changing cultural and financial patterns. The ascent of social business, for instance, has carried another aspect to the startup world. Social business visionaries plan to make organizations that produce benefits as well as address squeezing social and ecological issues. They look to have a constructive outcome on the world while maintaining a manageable business.

The idea of effect money management, which centers around supporting organizations that make both monetary returns and positive social or natural results, has gotten momentum. This pattern highlights that new businesses can be influencers, resolving issues like environmental change, destitution, and imbalance while chasing after productivity.

Moreover, the worldwide scene of business venture has become progressively interconnected. New companies never again work in separation; they are essential for a worldwide biological system. They can get to assets, ability, and markets on a worldwide scale, because of the web and computerized stages. This interconnectedness has opened up additional opportunities for coordinated effort, extension, and cross-line development.

In this interconnected world, the startup venture has taken on a more different and comprehensive person. The boundaries to section for underrepresented gatherings, including ladies and minority business people, have step by step disintegrated. Drives and associations have arisen to help variety in business venture, perceiving the undiscovered capacity and ability that can drive advancement and monetary development.

The job of government arrangements and backing in cultivating business can't be put into words. Numerous nations have executed arrangements to support startup development through charge impetuses, awards, and administrative changes. These drives expect to establish a helpful climate for development and business, perceiving that new companies can be strong drivers of financial turn of events and occupation creation.

While new businesses address the soul of advancement and the commitment of financial development, they are not without their faultfinders. The "flop quick, bomb frequently" mantra, normal in the startup world, has drawn its reasonable portion of analysis for advancing a culture of carelessness and inefficiency. Some contend that the accentuation on development no matter what can prompt untrustworthy practices, like information protection infringement and abuse of laborers.

The gig economy, frequently connected with new companies in the sharing economy, affects laborers' freedoms and employer stability. Adjusting the advantages of advancement with moral contemplations stays a continuous test.

All in all, the startup venture, from the origination of a plan to enterprising victory, is a story that epitomizes the quintessence of human desire, development, and assurance. It is an excursion set apart by dangers, difficulties, and vulnerabilities, yet additionally by the potential for pivotal achievement and enduring effect.

The appeal of new companies lies in their capacity to disturb business as usual, make new business sectors, and challenge laid out standards. They are vehicles for transforming thoughts into the real world and reshaping businesses. As we keep on seeing the advancement of business in the computerized age, the startup venture is turning out to be more different, comprehensive, and all around the world interconnected.

An excursion requests strength, versatility, and a readiness to embrace risk. An excursion blossoms with development and is frequently portrayed by asset shortage, profound ups and downs, and the requirement for mentorship and joint effort. Eventually, the startup venture is a demonstration of the persevering through soul of business, and it fills in as an image of the vast potential outcomes that can be acknowledged with the right thought, the right group, and enduring assurance.

1. **The allure of entrepreneurship**

   Business venture, with its commitment of freedom, development, and potential for monetary prize, has consistently held a special charm. The idea of making and dealing with one's business, of working for oneself, has for quite some time been a fantasy for some. In any case, the idea of business venture isn't just about getting away from the unbending nature of customary business; it addresses a significant change by they way we view work, riches, and individual satisfaction. At its center, business venture epitomizes the soul of self-assurance. Business visionaries manufacture their ways, characterize their objectives, and decide their fate. This feeling of independence, the opportunity to diagram one's course, is one of the central attractions of business. It is a definitive dismissal of the state of affairs, the conviction that people can shape their prospects as indicated by their fantasies and desires.

   The appeal of business venture rises above monetary profit. While the potential for monetary achievement is without a doubt a propelling element, the substance of business goes past riches. It's tied in with making, improving, and having an effect. Business visionaries, in their quest for building something significant, frequently find that their work turns into an ongoing source of both blessing and pain.

   Development is at the core of business venture. The main thrust moves people to take the jump and begin their organizations. Innovative endeavors, whether they include sending off a tech startup, opening a nearby pastry shop, or offering an interesting support, are driven by the longing to tackle issues or address neglected issues. This inventive motivation leads to new items, administrations, and plans of action.

   Business visionaries are, commonly, daring people. They will step outside their usual ranges of familiarity, challenge show, and face vulnerability head-on. The excitement of hazard, the fervor of venturing into the obscure, is a strong inspiration. It is this readiness to embrace vulnerability that frequently prompts pivotal developments and groundbreaking changes in different businesses.

   The computerized age has added another layer to the charm of business. Innovation and the web have democratized business venture, making it more open than any other time in recent memory. This openness has led to another type of business people, frequently alluded to as "computerized business people." These people influence advanced apparatuses, online stages, and internet business to begin and scale organizations. The web, with its huge reach and low section obstructions, has empowered a worldwide pioneering biological system.

The appeal of advanced business is irrefutable. The capacity to contact a worldwide crowd, frequently from the solace of one's home, has opened up a universe of conceivable outcomes. Online organizations, from internet business stores to content creation stages, offer adaptability, versatility, and the potential for significant pay. This shift towards advanced business has reclassified conventional ideas of work and vocation.

One of the vital elements of advanced business is the idea of the "side gig." Numerous people, while holding down conventional positions, seek after innovative undertakings as an afterthought. This equal quest for business venture gives monetary security while permitting people to investigate their interests and possibly change into full-time business venture.

The charm of advanced business venture lies in its adaptability. It permits people to plan their work around their ways of life, instead of the opposite way around. The capacity to work from a distance, set up one's schedule, and decide one's workplace has changed the manner in which we see work. This change provokes the conventional all day office model and enables people to focus on balance between fun and serious activities and individual satisfaction.

Outsourcing is one more aspect of the advanced business scene. Consultants offer their abilities and administrations on an undertaking premise, frequently through web-based stages. This gig economy, portrayed by transient agreements and free work courses of action, has filled essentially lately. It permits people to adapt their ability, fabricate portfolios, and extend their expert organizations.

The appeal of outsourcing is established in the opportunity it gives. Specialists can pick the ventures they work on, set their rates, and, surprisingly, select their clients. This adaptability enables people to assume command over their vocations and spotlight on regions that really interest them. It's an option in contrast to the customary vocation stepping stool, where advancements and employer stability are much of not entirely set in stone by outer variables.

The gig economy likewise works with what is known as the "advanced migrant" way of life. Advanced migrants are people who influence remote work potential chances to travel and work from different areas all over the planet. This way of life requests to the individuals who worth encounters over belongings, permitting them to investigate various societies, cooking styles, and scenes while keeping up with their expert lives.

The idea of work-life reconciliation is a huge part of the charm of computerized business. Dissimilar to the conventional idea of balance between fun and serious activities, which frequently infers a severe partition of work and individual life, work-life joining recognizes that work is a key part of life. It urges people to wind around work, individual interests, and everyday life into an amicable and significant entirety.

The monetary compensations of business venture are an intense inspiration. Business people can possibly acquire pay that isn't limited by the imperatives of conventional work. The capacity to decide one's procuring potential is a strong motivator. While monetary achievement isn't ensured and frequently requires long periods of difficult work and steadiness, the charm of limitless procuring potential is a main thrust.

Enterprising examples of overcoming adversity, from carport new businesses to billion-dollar tech organizations, further fuel the charm of business. These accounts of poverty to newfound wealth ventures and troublesome developments catch the creative mind. They represent the possibility that anybody with a convincing thought and steady assurance can make noteworthy progress. The possibility of joining the positions of these examples of overcoming adversity is a fantasy that draws in trying business people.

Furthermore, business isn't restricted to a particular age bunch. While the picture of youthful, educated business people is conspicuous in the media, people of any age seek after enterprising endeavors. More established people frequently bring an abundance of involvement, industry information, and a solid organization to their organizations. Business venture can be a second, third, or even fourth vocation for the individuals who look for new difficulties and valuable open doors.

The charm of business additionally stretches out to the idea of social business venture. Social business people intend to make organizations that create benefits as well as address squeezing social or natural issues. These people are propelled by a feeling of direction and a craving to have a beneficial outcome on the world. The possibility that business can be a power for good, driving change and further developing lives, is a convincing vision.

Influence effective money management, a type of venture that spotlights on supporting organizations that make both monetary returns and positive social or natural results, lines up with the idea of social business. Influence financial backers try to convey their capital in a
manner that advances a superior world, resolving issues like destitution, environmental change, and disparity. This approach reclassifies the job of cash in business venture, featuring the potential for benefit and reason to coincide.

In the pioneering scene, mentorship assumes a critical part. Experienced business visionaries and business pioneers frequently share their insight, bits of knowledge, and guidance with yearning business people. Mentorship can give direction on exploring the intricacies of beginning and maintaining a business, offer answers for normal difficulties, and give admittance to significant organizations.

Mentorship is particularly essential for people from underrepresented gatherings, including ladies and minorities, who face one of a kind snags in the pioneering scene. Drives and associations that emphasis on encouraging variety in business plan to even the odds and establish a comprehensive climate where all people have the chance to flourish.

Government arrangements and backing additionally impact the appeal of business venture. Numerous nations have carried out arrangements to support startup development through charge motivators, awards, and administrative changes. These drives plan to establish a favorable climate for advancement and business, perceiving that new companies can be strong drivers of monetary turn of events and occupation creation.

In any case, it's essential to recognize that business isn't without its difficulties and reactions. The "flop quick, bomb frequently" mantra, normal in the startup world, has drawn its reasonable portion of analysis for advancing a culture of carelessness and inefficiency. Some contend that the accentuation on development no matter what can prompt untrustworthy practices, like information protection infringement and abuse of laborers.

The gig economy, frequently connected with new companies in the sharing economy, affects laborers' freedoms and employer stability. Adjusting the advantages of development with moral contemplations stays a continuous test.

2. **The birth of an idea**

Thoughts are the beginning of all human advancement, development, and change. They are the flashes that light the blazes of imagination, prompting revelations, developments, and significant changes on the planet. The introduction of a thought is an intriguing and many-sided process that happens inside the profundities of the human psyche, frequently ignited by a different cluster of impacts and encounters.

Thoughts, in their most flawless structure, are the psychological builds that envelop novel ideas, answers for issues, creative dreams, or better approaches for grasping the world. These thoughts are like seeds, little and apparently unimportant, yet they have the possibility to develop into something significant and effective. The course of thought age isn't limited by limits or limits; a major part of human insight rises above social, social, and topographical limitations.

The beginning of a thought frequently starts with the human limit with respect to perception. We see our general surroundings through our faculties, and these perceptions are the unrefined substances of thoughts. Whether it's seeing the shades of a dusk, experiencing the intensity of an oven, or paying attention to the tunes of a melody, our faculties continually give us a variety of upgrades that become the structure blocks of thought. These tactile encounters collect to us, framing a supply of tangible information from which thoughts can arise.

Nonetheless, only one out of every odd perception prompts a thought. Thoughts are not simple impressions of the world for all intents and purposes but instead reevaluations, associations, and new points of view on it. The basic component in this cycle is discernment, the capacity to see past the outer layer of things. A thought starts to come to fruition when one can observe examples, connections, and implications in the crude information of tangible experience. This demonstration of translation changes information into data and, at last, into thoughts.

Interest is a main thrust behind thought age. It forces us to get clarification on pressing issues, to look for understanding, and to investigate the secrets of the world. Interest drives us to dig further into the peculiarities we notice and to draw an obvious conclusion regarding apparently unique components. In this sense, thoughts frequently rise out of a condition of marvel, an unquenchable craving to uncover the obscure and get a handle on it.

One more essential part of thought age is information. The more we know, the more we need to work with while making thoughts. Information is the establishment whereupon novel thoughts are assembled. It fills in as a kind of perspective point, permitting us to draw after existing data, apply it in clever ways, or challenge and develop it. The most common way of making thoughts is innately total, with each groundbreaking thought expanding upon the thoughts that preceded.

The amalgamation of thoughts is one more vital part of the inventive flow. Frequently, novel thoughts don't emerge in seclusion however are the after-effect of joining existing thoughts in creative ways. This mixing of ideas and bits of knowledge from assorted fields can prompt weighty revelations. For instance, the introduction of the Internet can be ascribed to the amalgamation of thoughts from software engineering, data hypothesis, and hypertext writing.

The climate wherein a singular exists assumes a critical part in thought age. Various settings, societies, and networks give remarkable boosts and points of view that can shape the development of thoughts. An individual submerged in an imaginative climate might be bound to create imaginative thoughts, while one encompassed by a culture that values custom and similarity might have a really difficult time breaking new ground.

Cooperation and discussion are likewise fundamental in the introduction of thoughts. Thoughts are not lone substances; they flourish in a social setting. At the point when people participate in conversations, discusses, and the trading of viewpoints, they can ignite each other's imagination, prompting the rise of novel thoughts. Joint effort Is in many cases the impetus for forward leaps, as it consolidates the information and points of view of numerous people to create arrangements and bits of knowledge that might not have been feasible by a solitary individual.

Luck, the event of lucky occasions or revelations by some coincidence, habitually assumes a part in thought age. Numerous well known developments and revelations since forever ago can be followed back to fortunate minutes. For example, the revelation of penicillin by Alexander Fleming came about because of an opportunity tainting of a bacterial culture. While luck can't be depended upon to deliver thoughts, it stays a flighty however welcome supporter of the innovative flow.

The introduction of a thought can likewise be a reaction to outside difficulties or issues. When confronted with a trouble or a need, people frequently attract upon their inventiveness to foster arrangements. The craving to defeat snags or make life more straightforward drives the age of thoughts. Development in innovation, medication, and various different fields has been prodded by the mission to resolve reasonable issues and work on the human condition.

The innovative strategy isn't direct; it is a mind boggling, dynamic, and at times muddled venture. Thoughts might carve out opportunity to develop, and their improvement might be impacted by a large number of variables, including individual encounters, feelings, and, surprisingly, ecological circumstances. On occasion, thoughts can arise full grown, yet on a more regular basis, they go through a course of refinement, transformation, and development.

Thoughts are not restricted to a particular space of human undertaking. They can be logical, imaginative, philosophical, or functional. A logical thought can prompt noteworthy examination, while an imaginative thought can bring about an immortal magnum opus. Philosophical thoughts can shape the manner in which we ponder the world and our place in it, and useful thoughts can upgrade the manner in which we live, work, and associate.

The capacity to make an interpretation of a thought into reality frequently requires a blend of assurance and reasonable abilities. Taking a thought from origination to execution includes cautious preparation, asset allotment, and critical thinking. This change cycle can be essentially as multifaceted as the thought age itself and is set apart by perseverance and flexibility.

The historical backdrop of development is rich with instances of extraordinary thoughts that have reshaped the world. The print machine, a thought that changed correspondence, is a demonstration of the force of development. Johannes Gutenberg's development made books more available, empowering the spread of information and thoughts on an uncommon scale. This innovative jump changed how data was dispersed as well as had significant social, social, and political ramifications.

The possibility of a vote based system, an idea established in the works of logicians like Plato and Aristotle, significantly affects the course of history. The possibility that residents ought to have a voice in the administration of their social orders established the groundwork for current popular governments. It is a demonstration of the persevering through force of thoughts to shape human foundations and values.

Logical forward leaps, driven by the introduction of thoughts, have reformed how we might interpret the regular world. The hypothesis of development by normal choice, proposed by Charles Darwin, presented a change in outlook in science and stays a foundation of current science. The hypothesis, conceived out of careful perception and investigation, has not just changed how we might interpret the variety of life yet additionally ignited significant conversations about the starting points of species.

The introduction of the web is one of the most extraordinary thoughts of the cutting edge time. What started as a tactical correspondence network in the end developed into a worldwide data expressway. This progressive thought, which interconnects billions of individuals and works with the trading of data, has reshaped the manner in which we live, work, and impart. It has made new enterprises, changed existing ones, and opened up a universe of potential outcomes.

In the realm of business and business venture, the introduction of a thought is much of the time the foundation of progress. Organizations like Apple, established on carrying easy to understand registering to the majority, have reformed businesses as well as fundamentally altered the manner in which we carry on with our regular routines. Consolidating innovation with plan style has brought about notorious items that keep on forming the innovation scene.

The idea of social business venture, a thought conceived out of a craving to address social and ecological difficulties, is reshaping the manner in which we view business and its job in the public eye. Social business visionaries, driven by creative thoughts, are utilizing the force of big business to impact positive change. Their endeavors address issues like neediness, training, medical care, and natural maintainability, giving new models to how organizations can add to everyone's benefit.

Thoughts are not static; they are dynamic and transformative. They can be tested, refined, extended, or converged with different thoughts. The course of decisive reasoning and discussion is an essential part of the development of thoughts. Society advances as thoughts are exposed to investigation, tried, and refined through scholarly talk.

The introduction of a thought frequently difficulties laid out standards and convictions. It tends to be troublesome, agitating, and, surprisingly, questionable. Galileo's thought that the Earth spins around the Sun, in disobedience of the predominant geocentric view, was met with wild resistance by the strict and logical specialists of his time. The crash between the laid out request and the introduction of a groundbreaking thought can make seismic changes in the public eye.

Thoughts can likewise be a wellspring of social and imaginative motivation. The introduction of a thought can appear in the production of a composition, a novel, a piece of music, or a film. Creative thoughts frequently convey complex feelings, investigate significant subjects, and give a way to people to put themselves out there.

3. **The importance of the startup journey**

The startup venture, with its innate dangers, challenges, and elating highs, is a groundbreaking encounter that assumes a vital part in the cutting edge business scene. New businesses are something beyond pioneering adventures; they are the motors of advancement, monetary development, and cultural advancement. Understanding the significance of the startup venture is essential in valuing its significant effect on people, networks, and the worldwide economy.

At the core of the startup venture lies the soul of advancement. New companies are established on the conviction that there is a superior method for taking care of issues or address neglected issues. They rise up out of the longing to rock the boat and disturb laid out ventures with groundbreaking thoughts, advancements, and approaches. This creative drive powers the driving force of progress and pushes social orders forward.

Development is the backbone of financial development. New companies present new items, administrations, and plans of action that invigorate rivalry and drive efficiency. They make occupations, cultivate a culture of learning and flexibility, and improve the generally monetary dynamism of districts and countries. New businesses are a wellspring of inventive obliteration, an interaction by which old and wasteful practices are supplanted by fresher and more proficient ones, prompting monetary progression.

In addition, the startup venture is set apart by its remarkable way to deal with critical thinking. Dissimilar to laid out undertakings that frequently depend on regulatory cycles and various leveled independent direction, new companies have the nimbleness to investigation, turn, and adjust quickly. This agility permits them to answer market changes, gain from disappointments, and emphasize on their answers, at last prompting development and refinement.

The startup venture addresses a proving ground for people's thoughts, assurance, and capacity to transform dreams into real factors. It is a cauldron of self-improvement, where business people stand up to their feelings of trepidation, self-question, and the persistent strain to succeed. This course of self-revelation and strength building isn't just fundamental for enterprising achievement yet additionally for self-improvement.

The capacity to continue on even with difficulty is a main trait of fruitful business people. The startup venture is full of vulnerabilities, monetary imperatives, and the approaching danger of disappointment. It requires unfaltering assurance and the psychological mettle to defeat difficulties. The examples learned through these difficulties shape the person as well as the personality of the venture.

The startup venture is certainly not a single one. It is many times a collaboration, where people meet up to rejuvenate thoughts. Building a strong and skilled group is a foundation of startup achievement. Successful cooperation, described by a common vision, shared help, and joint effort, changes a thought into a flourishing business. The relational elements inside a startup are fundamental, as they decide the association's way of life, hard working attitude, and its capacity to adjust and improve.

The startup local area, both locally and universally, is a closely knit organization of similar people who offer encounters, bits of knowledge, and best practices. This feeling of local area is fundamental for business people, as it offers help, mentorship, and admittance to assets. The eagerness to help and gain from each other is a characterizing element of the startup world, empowering hopeful business visionaries to explore the difficulties they face.

Mentorship is a priceless asset in the startup venture. Experienced business people and industry specialists frequently give direction and bits of knowledge to those at prior phases of their pioneering tries. Mentorship offers intelligence, information, and an important organization that can open entryways and offer imperative help. The direction of a tutor can assist business visionaries with keeping away from normal traps and advantage from the encounters of the people who have strolled the way before them.

The significance of mentorship stretches out past the down to earth parts of business. Coaches can likewise offer the profound help and necessary support during the violent startup venture. They offer viewpoint, consolation, and a feeling of having a place, which can be a wellspring of inspiration and versatility for business visionaries confronting the difficulties of business.

Admittance to financing is a basic part of the startup venture. New businesses commonly work with restricted assets, and getting the vital capital is in many cases a huge obstacle. Financing, whether through private reserve funds, advances, private backers, investment, or crowdfunding, is the backbone of numerous new businesses. It permits them to employ ability, foster items, and scale their activities.

Pitching to financial backers, frequently alluded to as the "brief presentation," is a significant part of the startup venture. Business people should convince potential financial backers that their thought merits backing, that their business has development potential, and that it addresses a significant speculation. The capacity to impart a convincing vision, show market understanding, and undertaking responsibility is critical. Fruitful pitching can prompt essential organizations and subsidizing that drive the startup forward.

Moreover, the startup venture is formed by the steadily advancing computerized scene. The computerized age has furnished new businesses with remarkable instruments and stages for advancement, advertising, and versatility. Innovation has democratized business, making it open to a more extensive scope of people and empowering worldwide reach. New companies in tech-driven areas have saddled the force of computerized innovation to make imaginative arrangements and reshape whole businesses.

The crossing point of innovation and business has led to another type of new businesses, frequently alluded to as "tech new businesses." These organizations influence state of the art innovation, information examination, and man-made consciousness to disturb laid out business sectors and make new ones. They are portrayed by quick development, enormous scope financing adjusts, and a worldwide reach.

The effect of tech new companies stretches out a long ways past their particular ventures. They are likewise drivers of financial development and occupation creation. Tech center points and development groups have arisen in different regions of the planet, drawing in ability, speculation, and assets. These center points cultivate a biological system that supports new businesses and gives a climate helpful for advancement.

Notwithstanding financial development, tech new companies are impetuses for tending to complex worldwide difficulties. From medical care and schooling to manageability and online protection, these new companies are creating arrangements that can possibly alter the manner in which we live and work. They are at the front of making a more interconnected, effective, and feasible world.

Also, the startup venture has advanced to incorporate the idea of social business. Social business visionaries are people and associations that plan to make organizations that create benefits as well as address squeezing social or natural issues. They are propelled by a feeling of direction and a longing to have a constructive outcome on the world.

The idea of effect money management, which centers around supporting organizations that make both monetary returns and positive social or natural results, lines up with the idea of social business venture. Influence financial backers try to convey their capital in a manner that

advances a superior world, resolving issues like neediness, environmental change, and disparity. This approach rethinks the job of cash in business venture, featuring the potential for benefit and reason to coincide.

The startup venture is an interconnected worldwide undertaking. New businesses never again work in segregation; they are essential for a worldwide environment. The web and computerized stages have opened up additional opportunities for coordinated effort, extension, and cross-line advancement. Business people can get to assets, ability, and markets on a worldwide scale, working with the trading of thoughts and the scaling of organizations.

This interconnectedness has prompted an expanded accentuation on variety and consideration in the startup scene. It is not generally bound to a particular segment or geographic area. Boundaries to passage for underrepresented gatherings, including ladies and minority business people, have steadily disintegrated. Drives and associations have arisen to help variety in business venture, perceiving the undiscovered possibility and ability that can drive development and monetary development.

Government strategies and backing likewise assume a huge part in cultivating business. Numerous nations have carried out strategies to empower startup development through charge motivating forces, awards, and administrative changes. These drives intend to establish a favorable climate for advancement and business venture, perceiving that new companies can be strong drivers of financial turn of events and occupation creation.

The startup venture, nonetheless, isn't without its faultfinders and difficulties. The "bomb quick, flop frequently" mantra, normal in the startup world, has drawn its reasonable part of analysis for advancing a culture of foolishness and inefficiency. Some contend that the accentuation on development no matter what can prompt unscrupulous practices, like information protection infringement and double-dealing of laborers.

The gig economy, frequently connected with new businesses in the sharing economy, affects laborers' freedoms and professional stability. Adjusting the advantages of development with moral contemplations stays a continuous test.

Taking everything into account, the significance of the startup venture stretches out a long ways past the pioneering domain. It is an impetus for development, financial development, and cultural advancement. New businesses are the motors of imagination, disturbance, and the improvement of answers for complex difficulties. They shape the manner in which we work, live, and collaborate with the world.

Chapter 1

Conception and Ideation

Origination and ideation are the seeds from which development and innovativeness rush out, bringing forth clever thoughts, creations, and extraordinary arrangements. These cycles address the beginning of human advancement, as they are the flash that lights the excursion toward forward leaps, whether in science, innovation, artistic expression, or business. Origination and ideation are not restricted to a particular space; they are all inclusive cycles that rise above disciplines, societies, and limits. Understanding the meaning of origination and ideation is fundamental in valuing their significant effect on the world.

The course of origination starts with perception. People are normally inquisitive, and our faculties are continually taken part in the demonstration of seeing our general surroundings. We see the shades of a dusk, feel the surface of a leaf, hear the tunes of a melody, taste the kinds of food, and identify the scent of a blossoming bloom. Our faculties gather a variety of information from our environmental elements, making a rich embroidery of encounters and impressions. These perceptions act as the unrefined substances from which thoughts can arise.

In any case, few out of every odd perception prompts a thought. Thoughts are not simple impressions of the world for all intents and purposes but instead understandings of it. This is where insight becomes possibly the most important factor. The demonstration of insight goes past simple perception; it is the understanding of tangible information to recognize examples, connections, and implications. It is through this demonstration of translation that information changes into data, and data, thus, turns into the underpinning of thoughts.

Interest is a main impetus behind the origination cycle. It propels us to clarify some pressing issues, to look for understanding, and to investigate the secrets of the world. Interest drives us to dive further into the peculiarities we notice and to come to an obvious conclusion regarding apparently irrelevant components. In this sense, thoughts frequently rise out of a condition of marvel, a significant craving to disclose the obscure and figure out it.

Besides, the course of origination is affected by information. The more we know, the more assets we have available to us while producing thoughts. Information fills in as a kind of perspective point, permitting us to draw after existing data, apply it in new and creative ways, or challenge and develop it. Origination, in numerous ways, is a combined cycle, with each novel thought expanding upon the thoughts that preceded.

Amalgamation is one more critical part of origination. Thoughts are in many cases not singular elements; they every now and again rise out of the blend of existing thoughts in creative ways. This mixing of ideas and bits of knowledge from various fields can prompt historic disclosures and novel arrangements. The cross-fertilization of information and the combination of thoughts from assorted spaces add to the wealth and variety of human imagination.

The climate wherein an individual dwells assumes a huge part in the origination cycle. Various settings, societies, and networks give extraordinary upgrades and points of view that can shape the arrangement of thoughts. An individual submerged in an imaginative climate might be bound to create imaginative thoughts, while one encompassed by a culture that values custom and congruity might find it more testing to break new ground.

Origination, nonetheless, isn't restricted to the singular's psyche. It frequently includes aggregate ideation and joint effort. Thoughts can be considered through the collaboration of individuals, as different viewpoints and encounters impact and join. Overall vibes can prompt the arrangement of thoughts that are more hearty, multi-faceted, and imaginative than those created in segregation. The aggregate course of origination is a dynamic and consistently developing peculiarity.

Mentorship is a fundamental part of the origination cycle. Experienced people and coaches give direction and bits of knowledge to those at prior phases of their imaginative undertakings. Mentorship offers intelligence, information, and an important organization that can open entryways and offer essential help. Coaches assume an essential part in assisting hopeful people with exploring the intricacies of their picked fields, offering exhortation, consolation, and associations.

Mentorship reaches out past the viable parts of ideation; it can likewise offer close to home help and inspiration. The way to understanding a thought is frequently loaded up with difficulties, mishaps, and snapshots of self-question. Coaches act as a wellspring of motivation, giving a consistent hand and a consoling voice during the violent excursion of rejuvenating a thought.

The trading of thoughts, coordinated effort, and discussion are vital to the origination interaction. Thoughts are not detached elements but rather flourish inside a social setting. At the point when people take part in conversations, discusses, and the trading of viewpoints, they can animate each other's imagination, prompting the development of groundbreaking thoughts. The elements of human communication establish a climate where thoughts can be formed, refined, and extended.

Besides, good fortune frequently assumes a part in the origination of thoughts. Luck alludes to lucky occasions or disclosures that happen by some coincidence. Numerous popular innovations and revelations since forever ago can be followed back to fortunate minutes. For instance, the revelation of penicillin by Alexander Fleming came about because of an opportunity tainting of a bacterial culture. While luck can't be depended upon to produce thoughts, it stays an eccentric however welcome supporter of the inventive approach.

The introduction of a thought can likewise be a reaction to outside difficulties or issues. When confronted with a trouble or a need, people frequently attract upon their imagination to foster arrangements. The craving to beat deterrents or make life more straightforward drives the origination of thoughts. Advancement in innovation, medication, and various different fields has been prodded by the journey to resolve useful issues and work on the human condition.

The innovative strategy isn't straight; it is a complicated, dynamic, and at times muddled venture. Thoughts might carve out opportunity to develop, and their improvement might be impacted by a large number of elements, including individual encounters, feelings, and, surprisingly, ecological circumstances. On occasion, thoughts can arise full fledged, yet more regularly, they go through a course of refinement, variation, and development.

Thoughts are not restricted to a particular space of human undertaking; they length science, workmanship, reasoning, and commonsense arrangements. A logical thought can prompt historic exploration, while an imaginative thought can bring about an immortal show-stopper. Philosophical thoughts can shape the manner in which we contemplate the world and our place in it, and down to earth thoughts can upgrade the manner in which we live, work, and collaborate.

Thoughts are not static elements but rather powerful and transformative. They can be tested, refined, extended, or converged with different thoughts. The course of decisive reasoning and discussion is a central part of the development of thoughts. Society advances as thoughts are exposed to investigation, tried, and refined through scholarly talk.

The introduction of a thought frequently difficulties laid out standards and convictions. It tends to be troublesome, agitating, and, surprisingly, questionable. Thoughts can possibly alter the manner in which we see the world and to reshape human establishments and values. The crash between the laid out request and the introduction of a groundbreaking thought can make seismic changes in the public eye.

The historical backdrop of development is rich with instances of groundbreaking thoughts that have reshaped the world. The print machine, a thought that changed correspondence, is a demonstration of the force of development. Johannes Gutenberg's development made books more open, empowering the spread of information and thoughts on an extraordinary scale. This mechanical jump changed how data was scattered as well as had significant social, social, and political ramifications.

The possibility of a majority rules government, an idea established in the works of savants like Plato and Aristotle, significantly affects the course of history. The possibility that residents ought to have a voice in the administration of their social orders established the groundwork for present day popular governments. It is a demonstration of the getting through force of thoughts to shape human organizations and values.

Logical forward leaps, driven by the origination of thoughts, have changed how we might interpret the normal world. The hypothesis of development by regular determination, proposed by Charles Darwin, presented a change in perspective in science and stays a foundation of current science. The hypothesis, conceived out of careful perception and investigation, has not just changed how we might interpret the variety of life yet in addition ignited significant conversations about the starting points of species.

The introduction of the web is one of the most extraordinary thoughts of the cutting edge period. What started as a tactical correspondence network in the long run developed into a worldwide data expressway. This progressive thought, which interconnects billions of individuals and works with the trading of data, has reshaped the manner in which we live, work, and impart. It has made new ventures, changed existing ones, and opened up a universe of conceivable outcomes.

In the realm of business and business, the introduction of a thought is many times the foundation of progress. Organizations like Apple, established on carrying easy to understand figuring to the majority, have altered ventures as well as significantly impacted the manner in which we carry on with our regular routines. Consolidating innovation with plan style has brought about notorious items that keep on forming the innovation scene.

The idea of social business, a thought conceived out of a craving to address social and ecological difficulties, is reshaping the manner in which we view business and its job in the public eye. Social business people, driven by imaginative thoughts, are utilizing the force of big business to impact positive change. Their endeavors address issues like destitution, training, medical care, and natural supportability, giving new models to how organizations can add to everyone's benefit.

Thoughts are not static; they are dynamic and developmental. They can be tested, refined, extended, or converged with different thoughts. The course of decisive reasoning and discussion is a basic part of the development of thoughts. Society advances as thoughts are exposed to examination, tried, and refined through scholarly talk.

The introduction of a thought frequently moves us to stand up to the obscure, the neglected, and the untested. It welcomes us to wander into strange regions of the brain and the world. It tends to be an impetus for change, an impetus for progress, and an impetus for the investigation of additional opportunities. The charm of the introduction of a thought lies in the way that it addresses the quintessence of human interest, imagination, and the voracious hunger for information and development.

1.1. The spark of inspiration

Motivation is a secretive power that lights the human soul, fills innovativeness, and pushes people to arrive at new levels of accomplishment. It is the main thrust behind craftsmanship, science, development, and self-improvement. The flash of motivation is a basic and widespread peculiarity that rises above social, geographic, and disciplinary limits. Understanding the nature and meaning of motivation is fundamental in valuing its significant effect on people and social orders.

Motivation frequently starts with a significant feeling of marvel and interest. It is the consequence of a profound appreciation for the magnificence, intricacy, and secrets of the world. From the class of a numerical condition to the complexities of a butterfly's wings, the world is loaded with striking peculiarities. This natural feeling of miracle is a strong inspiration for investigation and disclosure.

Also, motivation is personally associated with the demonstration of perception. It is through our faculties that we see our general surroundings. Our capacity to see, hear, contact, taste, and smell is the doorway to tangible encounters that become the establishment for motivation. These encounters are the unrefined components from which the human psyche builds its interesting dreams and bits of knowledge.

In the domain of science, motivation frequently emerges from the perception of normal peculiarities. Consider Sir Isaac Newton, who was enlivened by the falling apple to contemplate the laws of gravity. Noticing the stars and planets in the night sky propelled endless cosmologists and physicists to disentangle the secrets of the universe. These logical experiences frequently start with basic perceptions, yet they lead to significant revelations.

Creative motivation, as well, is much of the time established in perception. The play of light on a scene, the many-sided examples of a cobweb's, or the human structure moving can act as the impetus for making visual workmanship, music, or writing. Craftsmen look to catch the pith of what they notice and offer their extraordinary point of view with the world.

Motivation isn't restricted to a particular space; it can appear in various structures. It can take the state of a strong inclination, a dazzling story, a piece of music, a striking picture, or even a significant thought. For instance, the idea of a majority rules system, which has reshaped states and social orders, started in the philosophical works of old scholars like Plato and Aristotle.

The historical backdrop of science and innovation is overflowing with instances of motivation prompting weighty revelations. Alexander Fleming's fortunate disclosure of penicillin, which upset medication, was enlivened by an opportunity perception of shape restraining bacterial development. Albert Einstein's hypothesis of relativity was propelled by his thought of the way of behaving of light.

In the realm of business venture and development, motivation frequently prompts the formation of weighty items and administrations. Business people recognize neglected needs or trouble spots in the public eye and are propelled to foster creative arrangements. For example, the development of the cell phone was motivated by the craving to join correspondence, registering, and diversion in a solitary gadget.

Self-awareness and personal growth are additionally profoundly interwoven with motivation. Numerous people look for motivation from good examples and tutors who embody the characteristics, accomplishments, or character attributes they yearn for. The biographies and accomplishments of these figures act as a wellspring of inspiration and direction.

The demonstration of seeing the accomplishments of others can act as a strong wellspring of motivation. The examples of overcoming adversity of famous figures like Nelson Mandela, Marie Curie, or Steve Occupations can motivate people to seek after their interests, conquer difficulties, and accomplish their objectives. These accounts act as evidence that incredible achievements are conceivable, no matter what one's experience or conditions.

Motivation frequently starts a feeling of direction and a source of inspiration. It constrains people to venture out toward their objectives, whether it's beginning another business, setting out on an imaginative task, or rolling out a positive improvement in their lives. The quest for one's motivation can be an extraordinary excursion that shapes not exclusively one's activities yet in addition their character and healthy identity.

Also, motivation is firmly connected to the idea of inspiration. It gives the underlying stimulus that shows people a way of activity. The internal drive pushes them to work constantly, continue on through difficulties, and stay focused on their objectives. Motivation can be the fuel that controls the driving force of ingenuity.

As well as persuading people, motivation frequently fills in as a wellspring of development and imagination. It urges people to break new ground, question the state of affairs, and investigate additional opportunities. The longing to make, develop, and have an effect on the planet frequently rises out of a wellspring of motivation.

The innovative strategy, specifically, is profoundly interlaced with motivation. Specialists, scholars, performers, and pioneers frequently wind up in a condition of stream, where motivation powers their work. This condition of stream is set apart by serious focus, a feeling of immortality, and the inclination that thoughts are streaming easily.

The idea of the inventive flow is likewise affected by the environmental elements and climate in which people work. Innovative spaces that are intended to invigorate motivation can significantly affect the quality and amount of imaginative result. Many organizations and associations have embraced this thought, establishing conditions that encourage development and ideation.

Cooperation is one more impressive impetus for motivation. The trading of thoughts and viewpoints between people can start new experiences and imaginative arrangements. Collective vibes frequently lead to imaginative results that might not have arisen in singular reasoning. Cooperative undertakings, whether in human expression, sciences, or business, can be a rich wellspring of motivation.

Mentorship and direction from experienced people can give important bits of knowledge and bearing to those looking for motivation. Coaches act as a wellspring of intelligence and mastery, offering direction and backing to those setting out on their imaginative or pioneering ventures. Their encounters and information frequently act as a well of motivation for trying people.

Moreover, motivation can be a wellspring of versatility and persistence during testing times. At the point when people face obstructions or difficulties, the memory of what initially propelled them can act as an encouraging sign and an indication of their objectives. It can give the profound strength expected to beat misfortune and keep pursuing their vision.

1.2. Identifying market gaps

Recognizing market holes is an essential part of business venture and business improvement. It includes perceiving neglected needs, strange issues, or underserved fragments on the lookout and tracking down inventive ways of tending to them. Understanding the meaning of distinguishing market holes is fundamental in valuing its significant effect on the achievement and development of organizations.

Market holes frequently rise out of a misalignment between what is accessible on the lookout and what customers really need or want. These holes can appear in different structures, including item or administration lacks, estimating shortcomings, or underrepresented client portions. Perceiving these holes presents a chance for business people and organizations to make esteem and cut out a specialty on the lookout.

Market holes are regularly distinguished through a blend of perception, research, and decisive reasoning. They require a profound comprehension of the objective market, its elements, and the necessities of its shoppers. Business visionaries and business pioneers should effectively participate in market examination to recognize these holes and reveal open doors for advancement.

Purchaser conduct and inclinations are dependent on future developments, frequently determined by advancing cultural, mechanical, or monetary patterns. Market holes can arise because of these changes. For example, the ascent of remote work because of mechanical headways and the Coronavirus pandemic made new requests for items and administrations taking care of work space arrangements, online cooperation instruments, and psychological wellness support. Recognizing and benefiting from such changes in purchaser conduct is urgent for remaining significant and cutthroat.

Development and innovative progressions frequently uncover idle market holes. As new advances are created, they open ways to tending to beforehand neglected needs or difficulties. The appearance of cell phones, for instance, presented open doors for application improvement, changing the manner in which we convey, shop, and access data. Business people who distinguish and use these innovative headways can connect market holes and make effective organizations.

Business people and business pioneers should likewise watch out for arising patterns and industry interruptions. These can uncover potential market holes that were recently ignored. For example, the expanded consciousness of natural manageability has prompted a flood popular for eco-accommodating items and administrations. Organizations that line up with this pattern are addressing a huge market hole while adding to a more economical future.

Also, social and social changes can make market holes that are ready for development. Segment shifts, like the maturing populace, have prodded the advancement of items and administrations focusing on the one of a kind requirements and inclinations of more seasoned shoppers. Perceiving and answering these social elements can open ways to new business open doors.

Market holes frequently exist in businesses with laid out players. These holes might result from smugness, protection from change, or an emphasis on transient gains instead of long haul consumer loyalty. Business visionaries who can distinguish these shortcomings and give unrivaled arrangements can disturb and rethink markets, as exemplified by organizations like Uber and Airbnb.

Business venture is in many cases about shaking things up and rethinking existing arrangements. Airbnb, for example, recognized a market hole in the customary lodging industry by interfacing voyagers with people able to lease their homes or extra rooms. This inventive methodology tended to the requirement for reasonable facilities as well as changed the manner in which individuals travel.

Recognizing market holes requires proactive endeavors to remain associated with clients and their developing necessities. Organizations that participate in open and straightforward correspondence with their clients gain experiences into their trouble spots, wants, and neglected needs. This continuous exchange is an important wellspring of market insight that can prompt the distinguishing proof of critical holes.

Also, assembling and dissecting client criticism can be instrumental in perceiving market holes. Criticism from item audits, reviews, and client care cooperations frequently uncovers regions in which organizations can improve and advance. Paying attention to the voice of the client is a fundamental practice for remaining sensitive to advertise elements.

Business visionaries ought to likewise focus on arising client objections or dissatisfactions, as they can flag potential market holes. A common issue or challenge looked by countless shoppers can act as a warning, demonstrating a neglected need. Resolving these issues can prompt the production of inventive arrangements.

Statistical surveying is an essential instrument for distinguishing market holes. It includes the methodical assortment and investigation of information connected with market patterns, buyer conduct, contender exercises, and industry elements. Research strategies incorporate overviews, center gatherings, meetings, and information examination. Statistical surveying gives bits of knowledge into purchaser inclinations, market patterns, and possible open doors for development.

Contender examination is one more basic part of statistical surveying. Understanding what contenders are offering, their assets, shortcomings, and client criticism can assist with recognizing regions where a business can separate itself and fill holes. By evaluating the cutthroat scene, organizations can reveal amazing chances to give better items or administrations.

Innovation and information examination have fundamentally upgraded the capacities of statistical surveying. Huge information and man-made reasoning devices empower organizations to investigate immense datasets to uncover bits of knowledge and patterns that probably won't be clear through customary strategies. By outfitting the force of information, organizations can come to additional educated conclusions about distinguishing and tending to showcase holes.

Market division is an important methodology for recognizing market holes inside unambiguous client sections. By isolating the market into unmistakable gatherings in view of qualities like socioeconomics, ways of behaving, or inclinations, organizations can fit their items and showcasing endeavors to more readily address the special requirements of each fragment. This approach can prompt the disclosure of undiscovered open doors.

Distinguishing market holes is a continuous interaction. As buyer inclinations advance and businesses go through changes, new holes can arise. Thusly, organizations should keep a persistent obligation to showcase examination and variation to remain cutthroat and imaginative.

Business visionaries and organizations that effectively recognize and address market holes gain an upper hand in the commercial center. They position themselves as issue solvers, giving arrangements that meet certifiable purchaser needs. In doing as such, they construct more grounded client connections and encourage brand faithfulness.

In the high speed business scene, remaining in front of the opposition requires cautiousness and deftness. The capacity to distinguish and answer developing business sector holes is a critical calculate supporting development and importance. Organizations that persistently search out amazing open doors for advancement and improvement position themselves for long haul achievement.

1.3. The art of problem-solving

Critical thinking is a major expertise and a fundamental part of human cognizance and progress. It is the most common way of tracking down answers for difficulties, obstructions, or quandaries that emerge in different features of life, from the everyday to the complex. The specialty of critical thinking is widespread and rises above limits of discipline, culture, and setting. Understanding the importance and subtleties of critical thinking is fundamental for valuing its significant effect on individual and aggregate human undertakings.

The course of critical thinking frequently starts with the distinguishing proof of an issue or challenge. It is the acknowledgment that a circumstance isn't as wanted or expected, which sets off the need to track down an answer. Issues can shift in nature, enveloping issues in math, designing, science, innovation, workmanship, regular day to day existence, and then some. Whether it is a riddle, a numerical condition, a specialized breakdown, a plan blemish, or a private matter, the excursion of critical thinking starts with recognizing the presence of an issue.

When an issue is distinguished, the method involved with characterizing it and understanding its extension and limits follows. This step is urgent as it sets the establishment for the whole critical thinking process. Without a reasonable comprehension of the issue, finding a compelling arrangement turns out to be significantly seriously testing. An obvious issue proclamation defines the boundaries and objectives for taking care of the issue.

In logical and specialized critical thinking, the cycle frequently includes figuring out the issue numerically or thoughtfully. This step takes into consideration the exact portrayal of the issue, empowering an efficient and organized way to deal with tracking down an answer. It includes characterizing the factors, boundaries, and limitations that describe the issue.

Besides, understanding the setting in which an issue emerges is fundamental. Issues are in many cases implanted in complex frameworks or conditions that impact their temperament and expected arrangements. Context oriented mindfulness gives knowledge into the more extensive ramifications of tackling the issue and helps in thinking about potentially negative side-effects.

Critical thinking is innately inventive. It requires the capacity to think fundamentally, examine data, and create clever thoughts and approaches. Imagination isn't restricted to human expression; it is a principal part of logical, designing, and specialized development. The most common way of formulating imaginative arrangements frequently includes the blend of existing information, innovative reasoning, and the investigation of unknown region.

The subsequent stage in critical thinking includes the age of likely arrangements or techniques. This stage is portrayed by conceptualizing, thought age, and innovative reasoning. It might include the improvement of speculations, models, or potential situations. At this stage, the objective is to investigate a large number of choices without essentially focusing on a solitary arrangement.

In logical critical thinking, the definition of speculations and the plan of analyses or tests to assess them are fundamental parts of the cycle. Trial and error takes into consideration the assortment of information and proof that can either uphold or disprove the proposed arrangements. The logical technique, which incorporates perception, speculation development, trial and error, and examination, is an organized way to deal with critical thinking generally utilized in logical disciplines.

Notwithstanding the imaginative angle, successful critical thinking frequently requires decisive reasoning and logical abilities. It includes assessing the potential arrangements in view of their achievability, significance, and arrangement with the characterized issue. Decisive reasoning is an orderly interaction that incorporates examination, assessment, and direction. It permits people to survey the benefits and downsides of various arrangements and pursue informed decisions.

The idea of the issue frequently directs the apparatuses and strategies utilized in critical thinking. In science and designing, formal techniques, calculations, and numerical models are utilized to track down arrangements. In human expression and plan, imagination and feel assume an unmistakable part. The way to deal with critical thinking can differ, and flexibility is vital to effectively exploring assorted issue areas.

Besides, the capacity to use innovation and information is progressively significant in present day critical thinking. High level computational devices, information examination, and man-made consciousness have extended the extension and effectiveness of critical thinking in various fields. These advancements can deal with tremendous measures of information, produce experiences, and improve arrangements.

Cooperation and collaboration are fundamental in numerous perplexing critical thinking situations. In the expert world, groups of specialists from assorted foundations frequently team up to address complex difficulties. The blend of alternate points of view, aptitude, and abilities can prompt more far reaching and inventive arrangements.

Mentorship and direction can likewise fundamentally influence critical thinking. Experienced people and coaches give bits of knowledge and backing to those looking for arrangements. They offer insight, information, and a significant organization that can open entryways and give direction in exploring complex issues. The direction of a guide can be instrumental in keeping away from normal entanglements and profiting from the encounters of the people who have confronted comparable difficulties.

Besides, the profound element of critical thinking is frequently disregarded. The most common way of wrestling with difficulties can be sincerely burdening, prompting dissatisfaction, stress, and self-question. Profound versatility and self-guideline are fundamental for keeping a productive critical thinking mentality. The capacity to oversee pressure, keep on track, and stay versatile notwithstanding difficulties is an important expertise.

The quest for imaginative arrangements frequently requests ingenuity and versatility. Tackling complex issues can be tedious, and misfortunes are normal. The capacity to endure notwithstanding difficulty is a central trait of effective issue solvers. It requires unflinching assurance and the psychological grit to defeat deterrents and keep looking for arrangements.

The execution of an answer denotes a basic stage in the critical thinking process. It includes making an interpretation of the picked arrangement right into it. Execution requires cautious preparation, asset portion, and execution. Compelling execution is many times a proportion of the progress of a critical thinking try.

Assessment and criticism are basic to the critical thinking process. It includes evaluating the aftereffects of the executed arrangement and estimating them against the characterized issue articulation and objectives. Criticism helps in grasping the adequacy of the arrangement and distinguishing regions for development.

The course of critical thinking isn't direct or unbending. It is iterative and frequently requires returning to past strides as new data or experiences become accessible. Issues can be dynamic, advancing, and affected by outside factors. Critical thinking is a constant educational experience that advantages from variation and adaptability.

The meaning of critical thinking reaches out past individual difficulties. It is a main impetus in logical disclosure, mechanical development, and cultural advancement. A significant number of the world's most major problems, for example, environmental change, medical services, and neediness, require creative critical thinking on a worldwide scale.

In logical and mechanical areas, critical thinking has prompted noteworthy disclosures and progressions. The improvement of the web, space investigation, and clinical leap forwards are results of deliberate critical thinking. The cycle frequently starts with the distinguishing proof of a neglected need or challenge, trailed by inventive reasoning, trial and error, and coordinated effort.

In the business world, critical thinking is vital to item improvement, process streamlining, and market procedure. Organizations that can successfully distinguish and address market holes gain an upper hand. They position themselves as issue solvers, giving arrangements that meet certifiable buyer needs. In doing as such, they construct more grounded client connections and encourage brand reliability.

Also, cultural difficulties, for example, general wellbeing emergencies and natural issues, require worldwide critical thinking endeavors. Tending to these difficulties requires the cooperation of states, associations, and people from different foundations. It calls for inventive arrangements, informed navigation, and versatile techniques.

The specialty of critical thinking isn't bound to explicit disciplines or callings. A principal expertise engages people to conquer impediments, go with informed choices, and impact positive change. Critical thinking is a demonstration of human resourcefulness and versatility, filling in as a main thrust in the progression of information and the improvement of society.

1.4. The birth of a visionary concept

A visionary idea is the beginning of a pivotal thought that can possibly change the manner in which we see the world, carry on with our lives, or direct our business. It is an impetus for development, change, and progress, rising up out of a mix of creative mind, imagination, and a profound comprehension of existing real factors. The introduction of a visionary idea is a noteworthy interaction that has formed history and keeps on driving human undertakings. Understanding the beginning and meaning of visionary ideas is fundamental in valuing their significant effect on the world.

The excursion toward a visionary idea frequently starts with an individual or a gathering of people who have a one of a kind viewpoint, a sharp feeling of perception, and a profound interest on the planet. Visionaries are in many cases portrayed by their capacity to scrutinize business as usual, imagine conceivable outcomes past customary way of thinking, and perceive undiscovered possibility.

Perception is a major part of the visionary idea's introduction to the world. Visionaries have an increased consciousness of their environmental factors and are sharp onlookers of the world. They notice examples, inconsistencies, and open doors that could evade others. This capacity to notice and decipher the world with a new viewpoint is a sign of visionary reasoning.

Besides, visionaries are much of the time driven by a significant feeling of miracle and interest. They are enamored by the secrets of the universe, the intricacies of human way of behaving, or the undiscovered possibility of innovation. This intrinsic feeling of miracle urges visionaries to investigate the obscure, look for replies to the unasked inquiries, and push the limits of human information.

A visionary idea isn't restricted to a particular space yet can traverse science, innovation, human expression, sociologies, and business. In the realm of science, visionaries like Albert Einstein, who planned the hypothesis of relativity, or Charles Darwin, who proposed the hypothesis of development, tested existing ideal models and reformed how we might interpret the normal world.

In innovation, visionaries like Steve Occupations, prime supporter of Macintosh, imagined easy to understand figuring and made imaginative items that keep on molding the innovation scene. His visionary idea prompted the improvement of the iPhone, a gadget that has changed the manner in which we convey, work, and access data.

Artistic expressions have likewise been significantly affected by visionary ideas. Consider crafted by Leonardo da Vinci, whose imaginative reasoning and imagination in different disciplines, from painting to designing, established the groundwork for endless creative and mechanical headways.

In sociologies and business, visionaries like Mahatma Gandhi and Martin Luther Ruler Jr. pushed for civil rights, uniformity, and peaceful opposition, reshaping the course of history and motivating developments for change. In the business world, the idea of problematic development, as proposed by Clayton Christensen, has turned into a foundation of present day business venture and rivalry.

The introduction of a visionary idea frequently includes integrating information from different spaces. It is a course of coming to an obvious conclusion regarding apparently irrelevant fields and thoughts. Cross-disciplinary reasoning and the combination of experiences add to the wealth and variety of visionary ideas.

Information, in this unique circumstance, fills in as both an establishment and an impetus for visionary reasoning. Visionaries frequently have a profound comprehension of existing information, which permits them to distinguish holes, question presumptions, and challenge

winning thoughts. This information empowers them to expand upon crafted by their ancestors and take it higher than ever.

Visionaries likewise embrace the force of inventiveness and creative mind. They are not limited by the limitations of what is right now known or practical. All things being equal, they utilize their imaginative resources to imagine a future that is profoundly not the same as the present. The capacity to consider new ideas, to push limits, and to really ponder additional opportunities is at the center of visionary reasoning.

The climate wherein visionaries live and work assumes a critical part in the introduction of a visionary idea. Various settings, societies, and networks give extraordinary boosts and viewpoints that can shape the arrangement of visionary thoughts. An individual drenched in an imaginative climate might be bound to create inventive ideas, while one encompassed by a culture that values custom and similarity might find it more testing to consider some fresh possibilities.

The most common way of imagining a visionary idea frequently includes wrestling with complex difficulties and problems. Visionaries are attracted to issues that have evaded simple arrangements and have significant ramifications. They are unafraid of handling the hardest inquiries, and they frequently revel in the intricacy of the issues they try to address.

The quest for a visionary idea can be impacted by a profound feeling of direction. Visionaries are much of the time driven by a longing to have a constructive outcome on the world, whether it is by working on the human condition, progressing logical information, or changing enterprises. This feeling of direction gives the inspiration and flexibility expected to beat snags and difficulties.

Moreover, visionaries frequently perceive the transaction between the miniature and large scale levels of their thoughts. They comprehend how their ideas can have broad ramifications, influencing a particular field or industry as well as society in general. They handle the far reaching influence that their visionary ideas can make and are ready to explore the intricate trap of results.

In the domain of business venture, the introduction of a visionary idea is the foundation of development and business achievement. Business people frequently distinguish neglected needs, market holes, or problematic open doors that can prompt the production of visionary ideas. For instance, the originators behind Google, Larry Page and Sergey Brin, had a dream of coordinating the world's data and making it generally open and valuable. Their visionary idea prompted the advancement of the world's most broadly utilized web search tool.

The improvement of visionary ideas frequently requires a blend of different and united thinking. Unique reasoning includes creating a great many thoughts and conceivable outcomes, while merged speculation includes assessing, refining, and choosing the most encouraging ideas. Visionaries frequently move this way and that between these methods of reasoning, considering the investigation of various thoughts prior to focusing on the most convincing one.

Besides, coordinated effort and collaboration assume a huge part in the introduction of a visionary idea. Numerous momentous thoughts rise up out of the trading of thoughts, the cross-fertilization of skill, and the collaboration of different viewpoints. Visionaries frequently encircle themselves with people who can contribute integral abilities and bits of knowledge to their vision.

Mentorship is a fundamental part of the excursion toward a visionary idea. Experienced people and coaches give direction and bits of knowledge to those at prior phases of their innovative undertakings. Mentorship offers shrewdness, information, and a significant organization that can open entryways and offer imperative help. Guides assume a crucial part in assisting hopeful people with exploring the intricacies of their picked fields, offering exhortation, consolation, and associations.

The improvement of a visionary idea frequently requires a huge level of trial and error and prototyping. Visionaries won't hesitate to emphasize, test, and refine their thoughts. This course of experimentation helps in molding the idea and making it more hearty.

The introduction of a visionary idea isn't without its difficulties. Visionaries frequently face incredulity, opposition, and downers who question the plausibility or importance of their thoughts. The way to understanding a visionary idea is cleared with hindrances, and visionaries should exhibit strength and diligence despite difficulty.

Chapter 2

Strategic Planning

Vital arranging is a basic cycle that guides associations, organizations, and people in characterizing their objectives, designating assets, and outlining a course for what's to come. It is a fundamental system for going with informed choices, adjusting endeavors, and adjusting to the consistently changing scene of the advanced world. Understanding the importance and complexities of vital arranging is significant for valuing its significant effect on the achievement and manageability of tries.

Vital arranging includes a precise course of characterizing an association's main goal, vision, and targets and afterward forming methodologies to accomplish those objectives. This cycle isn't restricted to the corporate world; it is additionally significant in government, not-for-profit associations, and individual life arranging. Key arranging includes both the specialty of imagining an ideal future and the study of fostering an organized way to deal with arrive at that vision.

At its center, vital arranging starts with an unmistakable comprehension of an association's motivation, mission, and values. The statement of purpose fills in as the directing star, characterizing why the association exists and what it tries to achieve. The vision explanation expresses the drawn out desires, giving a distinctive image representing things to come the association plans to make. These assertions make a feeling of direction and bearing that shapes the whole arranging process.

The most important phase in essential arranging includes a thorough evaluation of the association's interior and outer climate. This evaluation, frequently alluded to as a SWOT examination (Qualities, Shortcomings, Open doors, and Dangers), distinguishes the association's ongoing position and the powers having an effect on everything in its biological system. It uncovers the association's interior assets and shortcomings, as well as outer open doors and dangers. This step is basic for a sensible and truth based arranging process.

Understanding the interior qualities and shortcomings assists associations with exploiting their benefits and address regions that require improvement. Associations need to use their assets and expand on them while addressing shortcomings that could block their capacity to accomplish their objectives. The outer open doors and dangers, then again, give the setting to vital choices. Associations should be ready to quickly jump all over chances and relieve dangers as they endeavor to accomplish their targets.

A critical part of the interior evaluation is figuring out the association's center capabilities. Center abilities are the remarkable qualities and capacities that put an association aside from its rivals. They envelop the abilities, assets, and information that give the association an upper hand. Recognizing and utilizing center abilities is essential for building techniques that are lined up with the association's assets.

The essential arranging process likewise includes setting clear and reachable goals. Goals are explicit, quantifiable, and time-bound focuses on that the association expects to achieve. These targets act as the waypoints on the excursion to accomplishing the association's vision. Goals ought to be reasonable and lined up with the association's assets and abilities.

Vital arranging isn't restricted to long haul targets yet in addition incorporates the advancement of transient objectives and activity plans. These are the noteworthy advances that an association should take to gain ground toward its essential targets. Activity plans ought to indicate the mindful people or groups, timetables, and assets expected for effective execution.

The portion of assets is a basic part of key preparation. Associations should settle on choices with respect to the distribution of monetary, human, and innovative assets to help the execution of their procedures. Compelling asset designation guarantees that the association can follow through on its essential goals effectively and economically.

In addition, vital arranging is an iterative cycle that requires standard observing and assessment. Associations should persistently survey their advancement toward key goals, recognize regions where course revision is required, and adjust to evolving conditions. This continuous criticism circle guarantees that the association stays responsive and dynamic in a quickly developing climate.

Key arranging additionally envelops risk evaluation and the executives. Associations should distinguish expected dangers and difficulties that could hinder the acknowledgment of their essential targets. Moderation methodologies and alternate courses of action ought to be created to address these dangers, giving a security net to startling turns of events.

In the corporate world, vital arranging is a significant device for driving development, overseeing rivalry, and improving benefit. Organizations utilize vital wanting to characterize their market situating, recognize valuable open doors for extension, and guarantee that their assets are designated proficiently. For example, Apple's essential arranging has been instrumental in laying out the organization as an innovator in the innovation business. The improvement of notorious items, like the iPhone and iPad, was a consequence of Mac's essential choices and asset portion.

In the public area, states and public establishments utilize vital wanting to offer productive types of assistance, address cultural difficulties, and advance monetary turn of events. Vital preparation in government centers around setting strategies, apportioning assets, and accomplishing long haul goals. For instance, Singapore's essential arranging plays had a critical impact in changing the country into a worldwide center for exchange, money, and innovation.

Charitable associations likewise use key wanting to successfully satisfy their missions and serve their recipients. Key preparation in charities incorporates characterizing the association's main goal, putting forth automatic objectives, and assembling assets to have a constructive outcome. For instance, the essential preparation of associations like Specialists Without Lines is vital in conveying clinical consideration to those deprived during philanthropic emergencies.

Vital arranging isn't restrictive to associations and establishments; it is additionally profoundly pertinent to people. Individual vital arranging includes defining objectives, deciding, and designating assets to accomplish a satisfying and reason driven life. People utilize key intending to explore their vocations, upgrade their abilities, and deal with their own lives really. This interaction is fundamental for pursuing informed choices, remaining focused with long haul yearnings, and making individual progress.

Powerful essential arranging relies upon a few crucial standards:

Inclusivity: Vital arranging ought to include key partners, including initiative, representatives, and important specialists. Consideration guarantees that assorted points of view and experiences are viewed as in the arranging system.

Arrangement: All parts of an association's methodology, including goals, activity plans, and asset portion, ought to line up with the association's central goal, vision, and values.

Adaptability: Brilliant courses of action ought to be versatile to changing conditions and new data. Associations should be ready to turn and change their techniques when important.

Estimation: Key targets ought to be quantifiable, permitting associations to keep tabs on their development and survey the viability of their systems.

Responsibility: People and groups liable for executing masterful courses of action ought to be considered responsible for their part in accomplishing the targets. Responsibility guarantees that activity plans are executed actually.

Straightforwardness: Correspondence of the masterful course of action, targets, and progress is fundamental to draw in partners and assemble trust inside the association.

The job of authority is foremost in the essential arranging process. Pioneers are liable for setting the vision, directing the arranging system, and it is actually carried out to guarantee that the brilliant course of action. Authority assumes a crucial part in adjusting the association, cultivating a culture of consistent improvement, and driving change when required.

Vital arranging is definitely not a one-time occasion; a continuous cycle develops with the evolving climate. It requires consistent checking and transformation to stay pertinent and powerful. Associations should consistently audit their systems and make changes in light of arising open doors and difficulties.

2.1. Market research and analysis

Statistical surveying and examination are basic cycles that empower organizations and associations to comprehend their objective business sectors, evaluate rivalry, and pursue informed choices. These practices are fundamental for recognizing open doors, moderating dangers, and remaining cutthroat in an always developing business scene. Understanding the importance and complexities of statistical surveying and investigation is vital for valuing their significant effect on the achievement and maintainability of ventures.

Statistical surveying is the deliberate course of social occasion, investigating, and deciphering information about a particular market, including its buyers, rivals, and other significant elements. An extensive and organized approach furnishes organizations with significant experiences to illuminate their methodologies and choices. Market investigation, then again, is the assessment and assessment of this information to reach significant determinations and make noteworthy suggestions.

The underpinning of successful statistical surveying and investigation is a profound comprehension of the objective market. Associations should recognize the socioeconomics, ways of behaving, inclinations, and necessities of their possible clients. This requires a mix of quantitative and subjective examination techniques.

Quantitative exploration includes the assortment and investigation of mathematical information. This information can incorporate market size, development rates, purchaser socioeconomics, and other quantifiable factors. Studies, polls, and measurable examination are normal devices utilized in quantitative exploration. For example, a dress retailer might direct reviews to decide the most well known dress styles among teens in a particular locale.

Subjective exploration, then again, centers around non-mathematical data. It digs into the inspirations, mentalities, and ways of behaving of buyers through techniques, for example, center gatherings, meetings, and perceptions. Subjective examination gives rich, setting explicit experiences that can be important for grasping purchaser opinion and inclinations. For instance, a product organization might lead inside and out meetings to investigate how clients cooperate with their item and recognize regions for development.

Market division is a key stage in statistical surveying. It includes separating the market into unmistakable gatherings in view of normal attributes or inclinations. These portions can incorporate socioeconomics (age, orientation, pay), psychographics (way of life, values, interests), or ways of behaving (buy propensities, brand dependability). Dividing the market permits associations to tailor their advertising endeavors, items, and administrations to explicit client gatherings, improving the probability of progress.

Serious investigation is one more indispensable part of statistical surveying. It involves assessing the qualities, shortcomings, methodologies, and execution of rivals on the lookout. By understanding the serious scene, organizations can recognize valuable chances to separate themselves and foster procedures that give them an upper hand.

Statistical surveying and examination are fundamental for recognizing market holes, which are regions in the market where customer needs are not satisfactorily met. Market holes can emerge due to developing purchaser inclinations, mechanical progressions, changes in guidelines, or changes in cultural standards. By perceiving these holes, organizations can situate themselves to fill the neglected requirements and profit by the amazing open doors they present.

Purchaser conduct examination is a pivotal part of statistical surveying and investigation. It includes understanding how customers settle on buying choices, what impacts their decisions, and how they associate with items and administrations. Purchaser conduct is affected by different variables, including social, social, mental, and individual viewpoints. By digging into these variables, organizations can tailor their methodologies to resound with their interest group.

Statistical surveying is a flexible apparatus that can be applied in different settings, including item improvement, estimating techniques, showcasing efforts, and development plans. It assists organizations with distinguishing which items or administrations are popular, how to cost them seriously, how to reach and draw in their ideal interest group, and where to geologically grow. For example, a tech organization might utilize statistical surveying to figure out which highlights clients need in their product, the amount they will pay, and which promoting directs are best in contacting them.

In the domain of development, statistical surveying assumes a critical part in figuring out arising patterns and customer inclinations. By remaining sensitive to these movements, associations can distinguish new open doors and adjust their development endeavors to advertise requests. This proactive methodology can prompt the formation of novel items or administrations that take care of advancing shopper needs. For instance, the ascent of remote work because of the Coronavirus pandemic provoked numerous organizations to advance in the field of working from home programming and administrations, satisfying the developing need for distant cooperation apparatuses.

Statistical surveying is additionally significant for risk appraisal. By investigating market information, associations can expect possible difficulties and dangers, permitting them to foster systems to relieve chances. Risk appraisal implies observing monetary markers, cutthroat turns of events, changing shopper inclinations, and outer variables, like administrative changes or natural movements. Organizations can get ready for the effect of these elements by going with informed choices in light of their examination and examination.

The approach of cutting edge innovation has reformed the scene of statistical surveying and investigation. Huge information, man-made consciousness, AI, and information investigation have opened up additional opportunities for social occasion, handling, and deciphering immense measures of information. These innovations empower associations to get important bits of knowledge from huge datasets, recognize examples, and settle on information driven choices. For example, internet business organizations use information examination to follow client ways of behaving on their sites and suggest items in light of individual inclinations.

Statistical surveying and investigation are similarly relevant to the universe of new businesses. New pursuits should direct careful exploration to figure out their interest group, evaluate contest, and distinguish market holes. For new companies, statistical surveying is instrumental in refining their plans of action, creating incentives, and getting subsidizing. Financial backers frequently expect new businesses to show a profound comprehension of their market and their methodology for entering it.

The act of statistical surveying stretches out past the business area. It is additionally fundamental for states and philanthropic associations. States use statistical surveying to illuminate approaches, evaluate the financial scene, and address social issues. Charitable associations apply statistical surveying to grasp the requirements of their recipients, streamline gathering pledges endeavors, and assess the adequacy of their projects. For instance, an administration might lead examination to decide the interest for public transportation in a particular locale, while a charitable association might accumulate information to comprehend the instructive requirements of underserved networks.

The most common way of directing statistical surveying and examination is certainly not a one-time exertion yet a constant practice. Markets are dynamic, affected by changing buyer ways of behaving, financial circumstances, mechanical progressions, and cultural movements. Associations should remain cautious and adjust their techniques because of these progressions to stay cutthroat.

2.2. Understanding the target audience

Understanding the interest group is a central part of successful correspondence, showcasing, and dynamic in different spaces, from business and promoting to training and public strategy. It includes a profound investigation of the qualities, inclinations, requirements, and ways of behaving of the particular gathering of people or elements that a message, item, or administration is planned to reach. Valuing the importance and subtleties of understanding the main interest group is fundamental for accomplishing reverberation, commitment, and outcome in any undertaking.

The ideal interest group is the gathering or elements for whom a specific message, item, or administration is planned. It can differ significantly contingent upon the specific situation and reason. In promoting, the interest group might be potential clients keen on a particular item or administration. In training, it very well may be understudies, guardians, or educators. In open strategy, it very well may be residents impacted by a specific drive.

Understanding the interest group is urgent in light of the fact that it helps tailor the message, item, or administration to be more pertinent and interesting to the expected beneficiaries. It guarantees that the correspondence reverberates with the crowd's necessities, values, and inclinations. Successful crowd understanding can prompt better commitment, reaction rates, and results.

One of the most important phases in understanding the interest group is characterizing its qualities. This incorporates segment data like age, orientation, pay, area, and schooling level. Socioeconomics give a basic comprehension of who the crowd is and what they are used to. For instance, an organization selling extravagance watches may target big league salary people with a particular age range.

Past socioeconomics, psychographics dive into the crowd's convictions, values, perspectives, and way of life. This data gives a more nuanced perspective on the crowd's inspirations and inclinations. It helps in creating messages and items that line up with the crowd's qualities and desires. For example, a not-for-profit association zeroed in on ecological protection could target people who are energetic about manageability and nature.

Understanding the interest group likewise requires a profound enthusiasm for their necessities and trouble spots. What difficulties do they face, and how could the item or administration address these difficulties? What objectives and wants rouse them, and how might the message or item line up with these goals? Identifying with the crowd's necessities and trouble spots is fundamental for creating powerful arrangements. For instance, a wellness brand could target people hoping to work on their wellbeing and prosperity, offering items and administrations that take care of their particular wellness objectives.

Conduct information is one more imperative part of figuring out the main interest group. It includes dissecting how the crowd collaborates with items or administrations, their buy ways of behaving, online exercises, and virtual entertainment commitment. Social bits of knowledge can illuminate promoting methodologies and assist with upgrading the client experience. For example, an internet business organization might utilize information on client perusing and buying propensities to customize item suggestions and further develop the shopping experience.

Understanding the ideal interest group is a consistent cycle that requires continuous examination and investigation. Markets and crowds are dynamic, and their inclinations, requirements, and ways of behaving can change after some time. Remaining receptive to these movements is significant for remaining pertinent and cutthroat.

Powerful strategies for understanding the main interest group incorporate reviews, center gatherings, meetings, and information investigation. Reviews and surveys can accumulate quantitative information on socioeconomics, inclinations, and ways of behaving. They can be disseminated on the web, by telephone, or face to face, contingent upon the crowd and examination objectives. Center gatherings and meetings give subjective bits of knowledge by permitting members to offer their viewpoints, inspirations, and encounters. Information investigation include gathering and examining conduct information, frequently from online sources, to figure out crowd communications and inclinations.

For instance, another portable application might direct overviews and center gatherings with its ideal interest group to assemble bits of knowledge on client inclinations and problem areas. It might likewise utilize information examination to follow client connections inside the application, like element use and meeting term.

Furthermore, understanding the ideal interest group frequently includes division, which is the method involved with partitioning the crowd into particular gatherings in light of shared qualities or inclinations. Dividing the crowd considers more exact focusing on and customization of messages and contributions. Division can be founded on segment factors, like age or area, or psychographic factors, like way of life and values.

Division can prompt fitted showcasing efforts that talk straightforwardly to every crowd section. For example, a dress retailer might portion its crowd by age, advancing various styles and items to teens, youthful grown-ups, and more seasoned people.

Social responsiveness is a urgent thought while figuring out the interest group, particularly in a globalized world with different populaces. Various societies have extraordinary traditions, values, and correspondence styles. Neglecting to recognize these distinctions can prompt mistaken assumptions or misinterpretations. Social awareness guarantees that messages, items, or administrations are conscious and applicable to the social setting of the interest group.

In the advanced age, online presence and virtual entertainment stages offer important bits of knowledge into crowd ways of behaving and inclinations. Virtual entertainment observing instruments and web investigation can give information on client commitment, content cooperation, and opinion examination. These instruments assist associations with following web-based discussions about their items or administrations, distinguish patterns, and measure the adequacy of their internet advertising endeavors.

Understanding the ideal interest group isn't restricted to the domain of advertising and business. It is likewise a basic component in the fields of public strategy and government. Government organizations frequently direct broad examination to comprehend the requirements and inclinations of residents impacted by approaches or projects. This crowd understanding is fundamental for planning arrangements that successfully address cultural difficulties and further develop the prosperity of the populace.

In training, understanding the main interest group is essential for planning educational programs and instructive materials that reverberate with understudies and work with viable learning. Instructors and teachers should adjust their helping strategies to address the issues and learning styles of their understudies. This approach guarantees that understudies are locked in and spurred to learn.

The utilization of understanding the interest group reaches out to the philanthropic area, where associations mean to resolve cultural issues and draw in with contributors, volunteers, and recipients. Philanthropies should comprehend the inspirations and interests of their different partners to make convincing messages and drives that resound with their crowds.

The idea of personas is a typical methodology in crowd understanding. Personas are fictitious, point by point portrayals of various crowd fragments. They incorporate segment data, inspirations, ways of behaving, and trouble spots. Making personas permits associations to acculturate their interest group and pursue more educated choices. For example, a philanthropic association zeroed in on youngsters' schooling might make personas addressing educators, guardians, and understudies, with every persona giving experiences into the particular necessities and inclinations of these gatherings.

Compassion is a focal component of figuring out the interest group. It includes setting oneself in the shoes of the crowd, seeing the world according to their point of view, and feeling what they feel. Sympathy cultivates a more profound association among associations and their crowds, taking into consideration more compelling correspondence and relationship-building.

2.3. Competitive landscape evaluation

Assessing the cutthroat scene is a crucial practice in business and vital arranging that includes surveying the qualities, shortcomings, open doors, and dangers introduced by rivals in a specific industry or market. This interaction is critical for organizations and associations to comprehend their serious position, go with informed choices, and foster viable methodologies. Valuing the importance and complexities of cutthroat scene assessment is fundamental for progress and maintainability in the present dynamic and speedy business climate.

The cutthroat scene is the unique biological system of organizations, associations, and elements that work in a similar industry or market. It incorporates both direct contenders offering comparative items or administrations and circuitous contenders that address comparative shopper needs yet with various arrangements. A thorough assessment of the serious scene gives experiences into how an association can situate itself decisively and flourish in an exceptionally cutthroat climate.

Understanding the serious scene requires an efficient methodology that incorporates a few key parts:

Contender Recognizable proof: The initial step is to distinguish and inventory contenders inside the business or market. Contenders can go from deep rooted enterprises to new companies, and they might have differing portions of the overall industry, assets, and procedures. Fundamental to make an exhaustive rundown incorporates every single expected rival, as ignoring even minor contenders can prompt botched open doors or dangers.

Contender Investigation: Whenever contenders are recognized, the following stage is to lead an exhaustive examination of their assets and shortcomings. This examination incorporates surveying their market presence, item or administration contributions, client base, monetary assets, dispersion channels, and evaluating techniques. Understanding the contender's plan of action and how they make an incentive for their clients is basic.

Market Situating: Breaking down how contenders position themselves in the market is fundamental. Market situating alludes to how a business introduces itself to its ideal interest group comparable to contenders. It incorporates factors like the uniqueness of an item or administration, evaluating technique, marking, and the apparent worth gave to clients.

Piece of the pie and Development: Inspecting a contender's portion of the overall industry and development patterns offers significant bits of knowledge into their presentation. Associations ought to consider whether contenders are acquiring or losing piece of the pie, and in the event that they are venturing into new business sectors or fragments. This information can uncover possible open doors or dangers.

Upper hand: Distinguishing a contender's upper hand — what separates them from others in the business — is essential. It very well may be their exclusive innovation, predominant client support, major areas of strength for a, or cost initiative. Understanding a contender's upper hand can illuminate procedures to either counter it or separate from it.

SWOT Examination: Directing a SWOT investigation (Qualities, Shortcomings, Open doors, and Dangers) for each significant contender gives an organized system to figuring out their inward and outer elements. Qualities and shortcomings are inner variables, while potential open doors and dangers are outside factors. This examination distinguishes possible areas of influence or weakness.

Client and Market Division: Understanding a contender's client base and market division can uncover regions where they might be defenseless. It likewise distinguishes holes in the market that could be taken advantage of to acquire an upper hand.

Evaluating Methodologies: Valuing techniques fundamentally affect contest. Understanding how contenders value their items or administrations, whether they utilize cost-based evaluating, esteem based estimating, or different methodologies, can assist an association with pursuing informed valuing choices.

Cutthroat scene assessment is a continuous cycle that adjusts to changes in the business climate, industry elements, and changes in contenders' procedures. Here are a few fundamental parts of cutthroat scene assessment in more detail:

1. **Contender Recognizable proof:**
   Distinguishing contenders can be trying in the present complex business scene. While certain contenders might be self-evident and notable, others might be arising new businesses or specialty players. It is critical to project a wide net while recognizing contenders and not limit the degree to a modest bunch of the most conspicuous names.

Contender recognizable proof can include utilizing different wellsprings of data, including industry reports, statistical surveying, online information bases, exchange distributions, and client input. Also, associations ought to effectively screen their industry or market to remain refreshed on new participants and arising patterns.

Understanding the serious scene may likewise include characterizing contenders into essential, auxiliary, and tertiary classifications. Essential contenders are immediate adversaries that offer comparable items or administrations to a similar interest group. Optional contenders might have a fractional cross-over in their contributions or crowd. Tertiary contenders could work in related businesses yet at the same time influence the market.

2. **Contender Examination:**

   Contender examination goes past just posting contenders; it includes diving profound into their procedures and tasks. A thorough contender examination ought to envelop the accompanying viewpoints:

   Item or Administration Offering: What items or administrations do contenders offer? How do these contributions think about with regards to highlights, quality, and evaluating? Examining the highlights and incentives of contenders' contributions can uncover experiences about client inclinations.

   Market Presence: Where do contenders work topographically, and what is their market reach? Understanding their geographic inclusion can assist with recognizing potential development open doors or regions where the association could concentrate its endeavors.

   Client Base: Realizing the client base of contenders, including their size, socioeconomics, and devotion, is fundamental. This information can illuminate client securing and maintenance techniques.

   Dispersion Channels: How do contenders circulate their items or administrations? Understanding their conveyance channels can uncover expected holes or open doors on the lookout. For instance, a direct-to-purchaser circulation technique might be not quite the same as one that depends on retail organizations.

   Monetary Assets: An evaluation of a contender's monetary assets, including income, net revenues, and capital speculations, can give bits of knowledge into their dependability and development potential.

   Evaluating System: How do contenders value their contributions? Is it true that they are situated as minimal expense suppliers, premium brands, or some in the middle between? Estimating methodologies are key signs of market elements and situating.

   Marking and Advertising: Breaking down the marking and promoting procedures of contenders can give experiences into their image character, informing, and client commitment.

   Understanding a contender's shortcomings can be essentially as important as recognizing their assets. Shortcomings can set out open doors for separation and acquiring an upper hand. For example, on the off chance that a contender battles with client care, an association can zero in on conveying outstanding client service as an upper hand.

3. **Market Situating:**

Market situating includes characterizing how a business introduces itself to its main interest group contrasted with contenders. It's tied in with conveying the special worth an association offers and why it is the favored decision for clients. Successful market situating requires a profound comprehension of the serious scene. An association should recognize where contenders are solid and powerless and track down chances to situate itself as the prevalent decision. For instance, an organization could underscore its client driven approach in an industry where contenders are known for generic help.

Market situating can be founded on different elements, including:

Item Separation: Featuring special elements or capacities that put an item aside from contenders.

Evaluating Methodology: Situating as a worth chief or premium supplier in light of valuing.

Brand Character: Making a brand picture that reverberates with the ideal interest group and separates from contenders.

Client Experience: Giving an uncommon client experience that eclipses contenders.

Market Specialty: Zeroing in on a particular portion or specialty inside the market where contenders are less dynamic.

4. **Portion of the overall industry and Development:**

Dissecting a contender's portion of the overall industry and development patterns can give experiences into their presentation and market elements. This data can assist associations with measuring their own situation and pursue key choices appropriately.

To evaluate piece of the pie, associations can utilize information sources, for example, statistical surveying reports, industry distributions, and fiscal summaries. Observing changes in piece of the pie over the long haul can uncover drifts and recognize contenders who are acquiring or losing ground.

Understanding development patterns is similarly indispensable. Associations ought to take a gander at how contenders are extending, whether through new item contributions, geographic development, or market enhancement. For instance, a contender's introduction to another market fragment could flag a chance for different organizations or a possible danger.

5. **Upper hand:**

Upper hand is the interesting strength or capacity that separates a business from contenders and permits it to outflank them. Understanding a contender's upper hand is critical for associations trying to counter it or separate themselves really.

2.4. Crafting a viable business model

A feasible plan of action is the establishment whereupon effective endeavors are fabricated. It incorporates how an organization makes and conveys esteem, produces income, and supports its tasks over the long haul. Making a feasible plan of action is a key and inventive strategy that requires a profound comprehension of the market, clients, and the cutthroat scene. In this far reaching investigation, we will dig into the fundamental parts and rules that support the production of a solid and reasonable plan of action.

Understanding the Plan of action

A plan of action is an all encompassing structure that frames how an organization intends to work and create esteem on the lookout. It fills in as the plan for an association's exercises, giving a reasonable design to how it will convey its items or administrations to clients while accomplishing monetary supportability. The plan of action envelops the accompanying key components:

Incentive: This component characterizes the exceptional worth that an organization offers to its clients. It responds to the inquiry, "For what reason should clients pick our item or administration?" A solid offer tends to client needs and trouble spots while separating the business from contenders.

Client Sections: Recognizing and understanding the main interest group is critical. Client sections characterize the gatherings or substances that the organization expects to serve. Successful market division guarantees that the business fits its contributions to the particular necessities and inclinations of every client bunch.

Income Streams: A plan of action frames how the organization will create income. This can incorporate different adaptation procedures, for example, item deals, membership charges, permitting, promoting, or a blend of these. Broadening income streams can upgrade monetary security.

Channels: Channels allude to the different ways the organization will reach and draw in with its clients. This could include actual stores, web based business stages, direct deals, virtual entertainment, or associations with merchants. Choosing the right channels is fundamental for proficient client obtaining and maintenance.

Client Connections: This component characterizes the kind of connections the organization expects to lay out with its clients. It includes client care, backing, and commitment systems, from self-administration models to individual communications. Building solid client connections is fundamental for consumer loyalty and dependability.

Secret weapons: These are the basic resources and assets the organization expects to convey its incentive and work actually. Distinct advantages can incorporate actual resources, protected innovation, innovation, or human resources.

Key Exercises: Key exercises depict the fundamental errands and cycles the organization should perform to make and convey its offer. These can go from innovative work to showcasing, creation, and client support.

Key Associations: Organizations and coordinated efforts with different associations can upgrade the plan of action. Key accomplices might give admittance to assets, appropriation channels, ability, or correlative items and administrations.

Cost Design: The expense structure frames the different costs the organization will cause while working its plan of action. This incorporates both fixed costs (like lease, pay rates, and above) and variable expenses (like creation, promoting, and circulation costs).

The Development of Plans of action

Plans of action are not static; they develop after some time because of changing economic situations, client ways of behaving, and innovative headways. Organizations that stay light-footed and versatile in their methodology are better situated to flourish notwithstanding developing difficulties and amazing open doors. How about we investigate a few critical patterns and factors driving the development of plans of action.

Computerized Change: The multiplication of advanced innovations has changed numerous enterprises. Organizations are progressively utilizing computerized devices and stages to smooth out tasks, arrive at a worldwide client base, and proposition creative items and administrations. Computerized change has likewise led to new plans of action, for example, membership based programming as a help (SaaS) and stage as-a-administration (PaaS) models.

Online business and Omnichannel Retail: The development of internet business has reshaped conventional retail models. Many organizations have embraced omnichannel methodologies, permitting clients to shop on the web, in actual stores, or through portable applications. This shift expects organizations to deal with a consistent client experience across different channels.

Sharing Economy: The sharing economy plan of action, promoted by organizations like Uber and Airbnb, has upset conventional enterprises. It permits people to share assets, like transportation or facilities, with others for an expense. This shared model has acquired noticeable quality in areas like transportation, cordiality, and even apparatus rentals.

Membership Based Models: Membership based plans of action are pervasive in different businesses, including media, programming, and customer products. Memberships offer repeating income streams and encourage client faithfulness. They can appear as month to month or yearly participations, giving admittance to content or administrations.

Round Economy: The round economy model spotlights on supportability and lessening waste. It underlines reusing, reusing, and reusing materials and items. Organizations embracing this model plan to limit their ecological effect while making esteem through asset productivity.

Freemium Models: Freemium is a half and half model that offers fundamental administrations for nothing while at the same time charging for premium elements or content. This approach permits organizations to draw in an expansive client base and upsell premium administrations to a subset of clients. It is regularly utilized in programming applications and content stages.

Personalization and Information Driven Models: Organizations progressively use information examination to customize client encounters. Personalization upgrades client commitment by fitting item suggestions, content, and promoting messages to individual inclinations.

Stage Based Models: Stages interface various client gatherings, like purchasers and venders, and work with exchanges or communications. Organizations like Amazon, Alibaba, and Airbnb have become prevailing players in their separate businesses by making flourishing biological systems.

Key Standards for Making a Suitable Plan of action

Making a feasible plan of action is a diverse interaction that requires vital reasoning, a profound comprehension of market elements, and progressing transformation. A few key standards guide the turn of events and refinement of fruitful plans of action:

Client Driven Concentration: A client driven approach is essential to making a suitable plan of action. Understanding client needs, inclinations, and trouble spots is the establishment for planning a convincing incentive. Standard input from clients and statistical surveying can illuminate the model's development.

Separation: A solid plan of action ought to separate the organization from its rivals. This might include offering a remarkable item or administration, giving uncommon client care, or taking on imaginative estimating systems. Separation makes an upper hand and draws in clients.

Maintainability: The plan of action ought to be monetarily reasonable in the long haul. This requires cautious thought of income streams, cost design, and productivity. Guaranteeing a positive income and the capacity to cover costs is fundamental for business suitability.

Adaptability and Flexibility: Plans of action should be adaptable and versatile to oblige changes on the lookout, client ways of behaving, and arising patterns. Organizations that can turn rapidly in light of new open doors or difficulties are bound to succeed.

Esteem Advancement: Worth development includes conveying worth to clients in manners that are novel and unrivaled on the lookout. It frequently brings about the production of blue seas, or uncontested market spaces, where rivalry is insignificant. Organizations ought to endeavor to improve by they way they convey esteem.

Adaptation Techniques: Income age is a basic part of a plan of action. Critical to choose fitting adaptation techniques line up with the offer and client assumptions. Organizations ought to assess estimating models, like one-time deals, memberships, freemium, or publicizing income.

Environment Building: Building organizations and biological systems can upgrade the worth a business gives. Coordinated efforts with providers, wholesalers, and correlative specialist organizations can extend the scope of contributions and make an organization impact that benefits clients.

Information Use: Utilizing information and examination is progressively significant in present day plans of action. Information can illuminate direction, customize client encounters, and drive functional efficiencies. Organizations ought to put resources into information abilities and protection contemplations.

Versatility: A suitable plan of action ought to be adaptable, permitting the organization to develop without relatively inflating costs. Versatility is especially basic for new companies and organizations with development aspirations.

Chapter 3

From Vision to Reality

In the archives of mankind's set of experiences, barely any powers have demonstrated as strong, as otherworldly, as the force of vision. The dauntless drive of people to envision, to imagine, and to bring those contemplations into unmistakable presence is a sign of our animal varieties. A power has driven development, supported creativity, and molded the actual texture of our reality. This power has birthed domains and human advancements, motivated unrests and disclosures, and prompted the absolute most significant accomplishments in science and workmanship.

The force of vision isn't bound to the domain of dreams or dream. It reaches out a long ways past that, infiltrating the center of our existence. A power has moved us from the stone age to the space age, from the crude to the complex, from simple endurance to investigation. From vision to the real world, this excursion is a story of desire, assurance, and determined pursuit.

Humankind's story, at its quintessence, is one of visionaries who hoped against hope, masterminds who considered addressing, and practitioners who thought about acting. From the earliest ignites of creative mind to the most amazing accomplishments of designing, we have reliably looked to make the theoretical concrete, the immaterial unmistakable. From the second early people gazed toward the stars and envisioned themselves among them, to the current day when we regularly send missions to far off planets, our vision has pushed us to grow the limits of what is conceivable.

At the point when we talk about visionaries, names like Leonardo da Vinci, Thomas Edison, and Steve Occupations ring a bell. These people had not just the capacity to imagine an alternate world yet additionally the tirelessness to make their fantasies a reality. Leonardo's note pads were a demonstration of his complex virtuoso, where portrayals of flying machines and submerged investigation coincided with notes on life structures and craftsmanship. Edison, with his incalculable licenses, changed the world with the innovation of the phonograph, the electric light, and the movie camera. Steve Occupations, the prime supporter of Mac, upset the manner in which we communicate with innovation, giving us smooth and natural gadgets.

These visionaries, be that as it may, were not segregated figures ever. They were essential for a continuum, the inheritors of hundreds of years of human interest and development. They based upon the establishments laid by others and passed on their own heritages for people in the future to expand upon. In this sense, the excursion from vision to the truth is an aggregate undertaking, a multi stage sprint in which every age passes the light of progress to the following.

Vision takes many structures. It very well may be essentially as pretentious as imagining an idealistic culture or as modest as envisioning a dinner to one. It very well may be a diagram for a high rise or the plan of a recipe for a family dish went down through ages. The excellence of vision lies in its comprehensiveness. It isn't the sole space of the tip top or the informed. It is an inborn nature of the human brain, available to all. The flash lights the human soul and drives us to arrive at past our limits.

Since forever ago, visionaries have frequently needed to battle with cynics, skeptics, and hindrances. The way from vision to the truth is seldom smooth. It is loaded with difficulties, mishaps, and disappointments. However, exactly these obstacles test the strength of visionaries. They should gather their inward strength, flexibility, and relentless confidence in their vision to proceed, even despite misfortune.

One of the most astounding parts of the excursion from vision to the truth is the job of good fortune. A large number of the best disclosures and developments have been the consequence of surprising spots of destiny. Take, for instance, Alexander Fleming's revelation of penicillin. It was a fortunate occasion, a coincidental pollution of a petri dish, that prompted the improvement of perhaps of the main anti-microbial in clinical history. For this situation, vision met luck, and together they changed the universe of medication.

Additionally, the improvement of the Internet by Sir Tim Berners-Lee is one more story of good fortune. Berners-Lee's vision of a worldwide data sharing framework was acknowledged through a mix of his imaginative thoughts and the current foundation of the web. His vision crossed with the innovation of the time, bringing about an upset in correspondence and data scattering.

The excursion from vision to the truth is likewise set apart by the impact of culture, society, and the climate. Visionaries don't work in a vacuum; they are formed by their general surroundings, and thusly, they shape that world. The renaissance time frame in Europe, for example, was a rich ground for visionary craftsmen, researchers, and masterminds. The juncture of social, scholarly, and mechanical improvements in that time set up for the absolute most significant headways in mankind's set of experiences.

In the domain of science, Albert Einstein's hypothesis of relativity is a model of how vision can be formed by the social and logical environment of a time. Einstein's work was profoundly affected by the logical discussions and conversations of his time. He had the option to expand on crafted by ancestors like Isaac Newton and James Assistant Maxwell to figure out his notable speculations. His vision of another comprehension of room, time, and gravity was a result of his time and his exceptional viewpoint.

The excursion from vision to the truth is a demonstration of the force of cooperation and aggregate exertion. Hardly any extraordinary accomplishments are the consequence of a solitary person's work. All things being equal, they frequently require the commitments of many, cooperating towards a shared objective. The development of the incredible pyramids of Egypt, for instance, involved the work of thousands of laborers over numerous many years. The Apollo moon landing was the consequence of the planned endeavors of researchers, specialists, and space travelers, upheld by an immense organization of foundations and associations.

In the domain of workmanship, the cooperative idea of vision to the truth is obvious in the production of epic movies. Chiefs, screenwriters, entertainers, and innumerable different experts meet up to rejuvenate a story on the big screen. The many-sided movement of an expressive dance execution requires the synchronization of artists, choreographers, performers, and ensemble originators. These joint efforts change individual dreams into shared encounters that reverberate with individuals all over the planet.

The excursion from vision to the truth isn't restricted to the domains of workmanship and science; it stretches out to the universe of legislative issues and social change. Visionaries in these spaces have imagined an additional fair and impartial world and have worked resolutely to achieve that vision. Figures like Mahatma Gandhi, Martin Luther Ruler Jr., and Nelson Mandela are models of the force of a dream for a more comprehensive and merciful society. They confronted gigantic difficulties, including mistreatment, savagery, and detainment, however their relentless obligation to their vision eventually prompted huge social change.

In the domain of innovation, the progress from vision to reality has been especially groundbreaking. The expansion of PCs, cell phones, and the web has generally changed the manner in which we live, work, and impart. These advancements have their foundations in the dreams of trailblazers like Bill Doors, Steve Occupations, and Imprint Zuckerberg. Their dreams were not restricted to making items yet stretched out to reshaping whole businesses and social orders.

From vision to the real world, we have seen the advancement of innovation from room-sized centralized computers to take estimated gadgets that associate us to the world. The speed of mechanical headway is speeding up, and our dreams representing things to come are turning out to be progressively interlaced with computerized reasoning, augmented experience, and the potential for colonizing different planets. These dreams are not the stuff of sci-fi but rather are effectively being sought after by researchers, designers, and business visionaries all over the planet.

The excursion from vision to the truth isn't without moral and moral contemplations. As we tackle the force of innovation to reshape our reality, we should wrestle with inquiries of protection, security, and the ramifications of man-made consciousness. The advancement of new innovations, for example, hereditary designing and independent vehicles, raises complex moral issues that require cautious thought. The obligation of transforming visionary thoughts into reality stretches out to guaranteeing that these developments are utilized to improve humankind and the conservation of our planet.

From vision to the real world, the course of advancement is frequently interlaced with the goals of maintainability and natural preservation. As we stand up to the difficulties of environmental change and lessening normal assets, our vision for the future should incorporate a pledge to dependable and supportable practices. Visionaries in fields going from environmentally friendly power to preservation are attempting to guarantee that our dreams of a superior future don't come to the detriment of the planet.

The excursion from vision to the truth is likewise a demonstration of the getting through human soul and the journey for investigation. From the beginning of time, we have shifted focus over to the stars and the profundities of the sea with a feeling of marvel and interest. Our vision of what lies past our reality has prompted the investigation of room, the moon arrival, and the quest for extraterrestrial life. We have dove into the secrets of the remote ocean, finding new species and opening the privileged insights of our planet's set of experiences.

3.1. Building the founding team

In the domain of business venture and development, fabricating an establishing group is in many cases the main critical stage on the way to progress. The establishing group is the foundation of any startup or new pursuit, and its creation and elements can altogether affect the organization's direction. The most common way of building an establishing group is an intricate

and diverse undertaking, including a mix of vision, abilities, characters, and shared obligation to a shared objective. An excursion requires cautious thought, key direction, and a profound comprehension of the startup's goals.

The development of an establishing group commonly starts with a dream. The pioneer or originators behind a startup as a rule have an unmistakable vision of the issue they intend to settle or the open door they wish to seize. This vision fills in as the directing light, enlightening the way forward. It frames the targets, the mission, and the general heading of the endeavor. The most important phase in building the establishing group is distinguishing people who share this vision and are energetic about its acknowledgment.

Imparted enthusiasm and arrangement to the center vision are principal. An establishing group ought to be a gathering of people who are driven by a typical reason as well as display a profound faith in the issue they are tending to or the market they are entering. This common energy can act as a binding together power, assisting the group with enduring the unavoidable tempests that accompany business. While the establishing group is joined by a certifiable obligation to the vision, they are bound to stick with it and continue on despite misfortune.

The development of an establishing group frequently includes a sensitive difficult exercise. It is a mission for people with different ranges of abilities and foundations who can complete one another qualities and shortcomings. New companies flourish with development, flexibility, and genius, and this variety of abilities and viewpoints is a critical driver of progress. It's not just about tracking down similar people; about collecting a group brings a rich embroidery of abilities, encounters, and information to the table.

For example, in the event that a startup is centered around fostering another product application, the establishing group might require a blend of specialized mastery, plan and client experience abilities, and business discernment. These different abilities are fundamental for cover all parts of item improvement, from coding to UI plan to showcase system. It's normal for a specialized pioneer to cooperate with a fellow benefactor who works in business improvement and showcasing. This essential association unites the specialized ability expected to construct the item and the business intuition expected to take it to showcase.

Now and again, establishing groups may likewise look for people with area skill. In the event that a startup is entering a specialty industry or focusing on a particular market, having somebody in the group who profoundly comprehends the complexities of that field can be a huge benefit. This individual might have significant associations, experiences, and a nuanced comprehension of the objective clients' trouble spots.

Notwithstanding abilities and space information, the characters and working styles of the establishing colleagues assume a crucial part. New businesses are extraordinary and high speed conditions where adaptability, flexibility, and versatility are fundamental. Thusly, it's essential to consider how people connect with each other, their capacity to team up, and their ability to understand anyone on a profound level. A firm group serious areas of strength for with and critical thinking abilities is bound to explore the difficulties that emerge during the startup venture.

The significance of trust and open correspondence inside the establishing group couldn't possibly be more significant. Trust is the bedrock whereupon the whole undertaking rests. Originators should have the option to depend on one another to go with basic choices, handle difficulties, and work through conflicts. Transparent openness is of the utmost importance for settling clashes and keeping a sound working relationship. An absence of trust or viable correspondence can prompt the disintegration of the establishing group's union and at last imperil the startup's prosperity.

The beginning phases of building an establishing group frequently include a blend of prime supporters and early representatives. Prime supporters are ordinarily the people who share the underlying vision and contribute essentially to the startup's development. They are the people who face significant gamble challenges possession in the endeavor. Early workers, then again, may join the startup at a later stage yet at the same time assume significant parts in its turn of events. These early colleagues are in many cases drawn in by the capability of the vision and the potential chance to add to a developing organization.

The division of obligations among fellow benefactors and early colleagues is one more perspective to consider. It's essential to characterize jobs and obligations plainly to stay away from disarray and duplication of endeavors. For instance, one prime supporter might act as the Chief, answerable for the general methodology and administration of the organization, while one more might be the CTO, centered around the specialized advancement of the item. Early colleagues might play explicit parts connected with advertising, deals, or activities.

Value dispersion is a key part of building the establishing group. Choices about how possession stakes are designated ought to mirror the commitments, dangers, and obligations of each colleague. Value circulation can be a perplexing cycle, frequently requiring cautious exchange and documentation. Generally speaking, value circulation is attached to vesting plans, which guarantee that colleagues procure their possession stake over the long run. This approach mitigates the gamble of fellow benefactors or early workers leaving the organization rashly.

Building an establishing group likewise includes the thought of outside factors, for example, economic situations and contest. The planning of collecting the group is basic. At times, pioneers might need to approve their thought or foster a model prior to welcoming in extra colleagues. Notwithstanding, standing by excessively lengthy to fabricate the group can block the startup's development and upper hand. It is vital for Find some kind of harmony.

The enlistment of establishing colleagues frequently reaches out past the prompt circle of the pioneers. It might include organizing, going to industry occasions, and utilizing proficient associations with distinguish potential colleagues. The most common way of drawing in ability can be testing, particularly for beginning phase new companies that might not bring the monetary assets to the table for cutthroat pay rates. In such cases, the allure lies in the valuable chance to have a huge effect and offer in the likely future progress of the organization.

Another component that originators should consider is the social spasm of planned colleagues. The organization culture is formed by the originators' qualities, convictions, and hard working attitude. Accordingly, it's crucial for look for people whose values line up with those of the establishing group. A solid social fit cultivates a feeling of having a place and responsibility among colleagues and can prompt a more firm and useful workplace.

The idea of a Base Reasonable Item (MVP) is much of the time key to the startup venture and can impact the structure of the establishing group. A MVP is a form of the item that incorporates the most basic highlights expected to address the center issue or need. The improvement of a MVP might require a particular arrangement of abilities and mastery, and the establishing group ought to be prepared to convey it. At times, this might mean welcoming on a specialized fellow benefactor or early representatives with the fundamental specialized abilities to construct the MVP.

The MVP is a significant device for testing the item on the lookout, gathering input, and approving the reasonability of the startup's idea. It gives a chance to learn, repeat, and refine the item founded on client input. The MVP can likewise be a significant resource while looking for financing or venture, as it exhibits that the establishing group is fit for executing on its vision.

As the startup develops and advances, the necessities of the establishing group might change. Extra colleagues might be welcomed on to help the organization's development, whether as architects, advertisers, salesmen, or different trained professionals. It is at this stage that the establishing group should adjust and advance to oblige the developing association's prerequisites.

3.2. Securing startup funding

Getting startup subsidizing is a crucial stage in the excursion of any new pursuit. A basic step empowers pioneers to change their inventive thoughts into substantial items or administrations, assisting with rejuvenating their dreams. Notwithstanding, getting the important monetary assets for a startup is a mind boggling and diverse interaction, impacted by different elements, including the phase of the organization, the market, and the sort of subsidizing looked for. Effective business people should explore this scene decisively, taking into account different choices and adjusting their methodology as their startup develops.

The startup subsidizing scene offers an assortment of supporting choices, each with its own benefits, necessities, and suggestions. These choices can extensively be ordered into bootstrapping, self-subsidizing, and outside financing. The decision between these supporting techniques frequently relies on the startup's transformative phase, its monetary necessities, and the pioneer's targets.

Bootstrapping:

Bootstrapping is a technique for self-financing where business people utilize their own investment funds or income produced by the business to support its development. This approach offers pioneers a serious level of command over their organization and limits outside commitments, like obligation or value circulation. Bootstrapping is especially normal in the beginning phases of a startup when the monetary necessities are somewhat unobtrusive, and originators are centered around item improvement and market approval.

Bootstrapping can be a maintainable methodology for new companies with a low capital prerequisite and a plan of action that produces income right off the bat. Originators frequently wear different caps, taking care of different parts of the business, from item advancement to showcasing and deals. This independent methodology empowers them to study their business and keep a lean activity.

A significant benefit of bootstrapping is that pioneers hold full possession and dynamic power. They are not obligated to outer financial backers, which can prompt a more elevated level of independence. This approach is especially appealing for business visionaries who are careful about weakening their value or surrendering control of their startup.

Be that as it may, bootstrapping likewise has its restrictions. The capacity to self-store the startup might limit the speed of development, as organizers are dependent on their own monetary assets. It might likewise restrict the size of the endeavor, as development frequently requires extra cash-flow to extend the group, put resources into showcasing, or foster new items.

Self-subsidizing:

Self-subsidizing is a variety of bootstrapping where pioneers utilize individual reserve funds, resources, or pay from their current business to back the startup. This technique permits business visionaries to infuse significant capital into their endeavor, possibly speeding up its development and improvement.

Self-subsidizing can be an appealing choice for organizers with a solid monetary establishment. It offers greater adaptability concerning the size and size of the startup. Business people who have collected privately invested money or have important resources might decide to use these assets to support their new pursuit.

One of the essential benefits of self-financing is that it empowers organizers to keep up with complete proprietorship and control of the startup. They are not responsible to outer financial backers and can pursue key choices independently. Moreover, self-financing can be a wellspring of pride for organizers, as it shows their responsibility and confidence in the business.

In any case, self-subsidizing likewise conveys extensive gamble. Business people are actually responsible for the monetary prosperity of the startup, and their resources might be in question assuming that the business experiences monetary difficulties. Also, self-subsidizing might restrict the extent of the startup to the pioneer's accessible assets. In the event that a lot of privately invested money is restricted in the endeavor, it might decrease expansion and increment monetary weakness.

Outside Financing:

Outside financing incorporates a scope of choices, including private backers, funding, crowdfunding, and different kinds of credits and awards. This classification of subsidizing sources acquaints outside capital with the startup, frequently in return for value or reimbursement with interest.

Private backers: Private backers are people who give cash-flow to new companies in return for possession value or convertible obligation. They are normally capable business people or high-total assets people who put resources into beginning phase organizations. Private backers offer monetary help as well as give significant mentorship and industry associations.

Investment (VC): Funding is a typical wellspring of subsidizing for new companies that have shown development potential. VC firms pool capital from different financial backers and convey it in high-development organizations. Consequently, they ordinarily get value possession in the startup. VCs can offer significant measures of capital, making them appropriate for new companies expecting to quickly scale.

Crowdfunding: Crowdfunding stages permit new companies to raise assets from an enormous number of people, frequently in return for item pre-orders or different motivators. Crowdfunding democratizes raising money, making it open to a wide crowd. This approach is especially engaging for buyer confronting items or ventures that can earn broad premium.

Advances and Awards: New companies can likewise investigate customary credits from banks, monetary foundations, or government-supported programs. Credits require reimbursement with interest, while awards, frequently accessible through government or confidential associations, give non-repayable financing to explicit activities or drives.

Getting outside financing is a complicated cycle that includes a few key stages. Originators, most importantly, should make a convincing pitch that really imparts their startup's offer, market a valuable open door, and development potential. This contribute is commonly introduced the type of a strategy, a pitch deck, or a financial backer show.

The subsequent stage is to distinguish possible financial backers or money sources that line up with the startup's business, stage, and targets. This might include organizing at industry occasions, utilizing special interactions, or moving toward funding firms or private backer gatherings. Online stages that interface new companies with financial backers, like AngelList or Kickstarter, can likewise be significant apparatuses.

Drawing in with financial backers requires powerful correspondence and discussion abilities. Organizers should be ready to respond to questions, address concerns, and present a reasonable guide for the utilization of assets. The reasonable level of effort process, which includes financial backers leading a far reaching evaluation of the startup's financials, innovation, and market methodology, is a basic stage in getting subsidizing.

The details of the financing course of action, including the value or possession stake presented in return for the venture, should be painstakingly arranged. It is fundamental for organizers to figure out the ramifications of the terms and to talk with lawful and monetary counsels when important.

Organizers ought to likewise know that various phases of a startup might require various kinds of subsidizing. In the beginning phases, when the organization is approving its idea and fostering a base practical item, pioneers might depend on private reserve funds, bootstrapping, or private supporters. As the startup develops and demonstrates its practicality, it might turn out to be more interesting to investment firms looking for high-learning experiences.

The choice to seek after outer financing ought to be all around considered and line up with the startup's objectives and development direction. Subsidizing adjusts frequently accompany assumptions for development and execution, and pioneers ought to be ready to live up to these assumptions. While outside financing can give the capital expected to fast development, it might likewise prompt a weakening of proprietorship and a change in the organization's dynamic elements.

Originators ought to likewise perceive that the most common way of getting outside subsidizing can be tedious and cutthroat. Dismissals are normal, and it might take various endeavors to get the right financing accomplice. Perseverance, strength, and the capacity to gain from input are fundamental credits for business people looking for outside financing.

Whenever subsidizing is gotten, organizers should be tireless in dealing with the assigned capital. Planning and monetary arranging are basic to guarantee that the assets are utilized really and effectively to accomplish the startup's targets. Financial backers frequently anticipate straightforwardness and responsibility in the utilization of their assets.

3.3. Developing a prototype or product

Fostering a model or item is a crucial stage in the existence of any startup or imaginative undertaking. It's where the theoretical thoughts, ideas, and dreams begin taking unmistakable shape, and the establishment for future achievement is laid. The most common way of rejuvenating an item or model is a multi-layered venture, including inventiveness, specialized mastery, asset portion, and a reasonable comprehension of market needs. This stage frequently fills in as the litmus test for the reasonability of a startup's idea and imprints the change from vision to the real world.

Characterizing the Model or Item:

The excursion starts with an unmistakable meaning of what the model or item is planned to accomplish. This incorporates recognizing the issue it means to settle, the requirements it addresses, and the worth it gives to its clients. In the realm of new businesses, this is commonly framed in an item or undertaking brief, a record that fills in as a kind of perspective point for the improvement cycle.

The model or item's definition ought to address crucial inquiries:

What issue does it address? Understanding the trouble spot or need that the model or item addresses is basic. This gives an unmistakable feeling of inspiration and a reason for estimating its prosperity.

Who is the interest group or client? Distinguishing the target group helps tailor the model or item to their necessities, inclinations, and ways of behaving.

What are the center elements and usefulness? Characterizing the fundamental parts of the model or item defines the limits for improvement and focuses on assignments.

What is the remarkable offer? Articulating the one of a kind selling focuses and benefits of the model or item is fundamental for separating it on the lookout.

How might achievement be estimated? Characterizing key execution pointers (KPIs) and achievement measurements gives a structure to assessing the model or item's exhibition.

Examination and Approval:

Prior to jumping into the improvement cycle, directing intensive exploration and validation is significant. This incorporates statistical surveying to grasp the cutthroat scene, possible contenders, and market patterns. Also, client research distinguishes client necessities, inclinations, and trouble spots. Bits of knowledge from this examination can illuminate the plan and improvement cycle and increment the possibilities making an item that reverberates with the interest group.

Approval frequently includes making a Base Reasonable Item (MVP). A MVP is a stripped-down rendition of the model or item that incorporates just the center elements essential for resolving the distinguished issue or need. The MVP takes into account quick testing and approval with genuine clients, giving important criticism and bits of knowledge. The essential objective of the MVP is to approve suppositions and lessen the gamble of building a full item that may not find a market fit.

Plan and Client Experience:

The plan and client experience (UX) of the model or item assume a vital part in its prosperity. The plan incorporates visual components, like the UI (UI), as well as the general client experience. The objective is to make an item that isn't just utilitarian yet additionally easy to understand, stylishly satisfying, and lined up with the brand's character.

The plan cycle commonly includes wireframing and prototyping, which help in imagining the UI and client streams. Iterative plan and client testing are normal practices to refine the plan in view of client criticism. Client experience examination and ease of use testing can furnish bits of knowledge into how clients associate with the item and recognize regions for development.

Advancement and Designing:

The improvement stage is where the model or item comes to fruition. It requires a mix of specialized skill, coding, and undertaking the executives. Contingent upon the idea of the item, improvement can be completed in-house by a group of specialists, moved to an advancement office, or even fabricated utilizing low-code or no-code stages, contingent upon the intricacy of the undertaking.

The advancement interaction frequently sticks to a lithe approach, taking into account adaptability, flexibility, and iterative turn of events. Nimble advancement includes breaking the undertaking into more modest, sensible errands or runs, with standard testing and input cycles. This approach guarantees that the item advances as need might arise and advertise elements change.

The decision of innovation stack and advancement devices is a fundamental thought. It influences factors like versatility, execution, security, and the speed of advancement. Also, guaranteeing the item's code is spotless, viable, and proven and factual is critical for long haul achievement.

Testing and Quality Confirmation:

Quality confirmation (QA) and testing are essential pieces of the improvement cycle. Testing includes a progression of checks and assessments to guarantee the model or item works as expected and is liberated from bugs, mistakes, or issues that could adversely influence the client experience.

Testing can envelop different levels, including unit testing (testing individual parts or modules), reconciliation testing (testing the connection among parts), and start to finish testing (testing the whole item's usefulness). This thorough testing process recognizes and correct any issues before the item arrives at its clients.

Sending and Scaling:

When the model or item has gone through the turn of events and testing stages, it's prepared for arrangement. Arrangement includes making the item open to clients, either through application stores, web facilitating, or other appropriation channels.

Scaling is a thought for items that experience quick development or high client interest. Adaptability includes improving the foundation and engineering to oblige expanding traffic and use. Appropriately tending to versatility can assist with forestalling personal time, slow execution, and different issues related with high loads.

Information Assortment and Examination:

Information assortment and examination are fundamental for understanding how clients interface with the model or item. This information gives bits of knowledge into client conduct, inclinations, and regions for development. It can illuminate choices on refreshes, highlight improvements, and advertising methodologies.

Normal examination devices and procedures incorporate following client commitment, transformation rates, client maintenance, and heatmaps. The information gathered ought to line up with the KPIs and achievement measurements characterized toward the start of the undertaking.

Client Input and Emphasis:

Client input is a consistent wellspring of data for working on the model or item. It's fundamental to lay out criticism circles, whether through direct client correspondence, studies, or application store audits. Routinely assembling and dissecting client input takes into account iterative upgrades and guarantees that the item stays lined up with client necessities and inclinations.

Advertising and Advancement:

The improvement of a model or item is just essential for the excursion. Similarly significant is the means by which the item is showcased and elevated to arrive at its main interest group. Viable advertising systems incorporate substance showcasing, online entertainment, email missions, and website improvement (Web optimization). Contingent upon the item and crowd, paid publicizing may likewise assume a part in the promoting blend.

Item dispatches are huge occasions that can create buzz and interest. A first rate send off includes making a promoting plan, creating energy through secrets and sees, and organizing with powerhouses or industry specialists who can embrace the item.

Adaptation and Income Model:

The income model is a central part of the model or item. It characterizes how the item produces pay, whether through deals, memberships, publicizing, or different techniques. The evaluating methodology and income model ought to line up with the worth the item gives and the inclinations of the ideal interest group.

Backing and Upkeep:

After the model or item is sent off, it are fundamental for continuous help and upkeep. This incorporates tending to client requests, bug fixes, updates, and security patches. Ideal help and responsiveness to client necessities can improve client fulfillment and reliability.

3.4. Legal considerations and business registration

Lawful contemplations and business enlistment are fundamental parts of beginning and working a business. These components are basic for guaranteeing that a business works inside the limits of the law, keeps up with its limitations, and lays out its authenticity according to clients, accomplices, and specialists. This complete conversation will dig into different legitimate parts of business, including enlistment, structure, contracts, licensed innovation, administrative consistence, and question goal.

Business Construction and Enrollment:

Choosing the fitting business structure and enrolling the business is quite possibly the earliest and most basic lawful moves toward laying out another endeavor. The decision of business structure influences proprietorship, tax assessment, risk, and administrative prerequisites. The most well-known business structures include:

Sole Ownership: This is the least complex type of business, where an individual works the business and is actually liable for its obligations and commitments. In many locales, no conventional enrollment is required, yet licenses and allows might be fundamental, contingent upon the business.

Organization: An organization includes at least two people who together work the business. Associations can be general organizations, where accomplices share equivalent obligation and risk, or restricted organizations, where a few accomplices have restricted responsibility. Organizations might require enlistment and a proper association understanding.

Restricted Risk Organization (LLC): A LLC offers an adaptable business structure that consolidates components of the two associations and partnerships. It gives restricted risk to its proprietors (individuals) and is a particular legitimate substance. Enlistment with the suitable state or purview is vital, and working arrangements regularly frame the organization's administration and tasks.

Organization: An enterprise is a different lawful substance from its proprietors (investors), offering restricted responsibility and the capacity to raise capital through the offer of stock. Companies require formal enlistment, and they are dependent upon more mind boggling administrative and detailing prerequisites.

S Partnership: A S Company is a particular expense assignment accessible to qualified organizations. It permits the organization to pass its pay, misfortunes, allowances, and attributes through to its investors for charge purposes, keeping away from two-fold tax collection. To fit the bill for S Company status, an organization should meet specific necessities and record with the Inner Income Administration (IRS).

The decision of business structure relies upon elements like the quantity of proprietors, the idea of the business, charge contemplations, and the longing for restricted responsibility. It is fitting to talk with legitimate and monetary experts to pursue an educated choice. The course of enrollment frequently includes documenting administrative work with the pertinent state or government office, acquiring a Business ID Number (EIN) from the IRS, and following nearby and industry-explicit authorizing and allowing prerequisites.

Agreements and Arrangements:

Contracts are the foundation of business connections and exchanges. A very much drafted agreement frames the terms, conditions, and commitments of the gatherings in question and fills in as a legitimate protect against debates. Contracts come in different structures, for example,

Buy Arrangements: Utilized for trading labor and products, buy arrangements determine the terms, cost, conveyance, and different circumstances connected with the deal.

Business Agreements: Work contracts frame the terms of business, including pay, work liabilities, advantages, and end provisions. They can be redone for full-time, parttime, or contract representatives.

Working Arrangements: Restricted risk organizations ordinarily utilize working arrangements to frame the administration construction, obligations, and working techniques of the organization. These arrangements give a system to how the business will be made due.

Organization Arrangements: For organizations, an organization understanding characterizes the jobs, obligations, benefit sharing, and dynamic cycles among the accomplices. It can assist with forestalling clashes and debates among accomplices.

Non-Revelation Arrangements (NDAs): NDAs, otherwise called secrecy arrangements, safeguard delicate data divided among parties by legitimately restricting them not to unveil or involve the data for unapproved purposes.

Administration Arrangements: Administration arrangements oversee the arrangement of administrations by one party to another. They indicate the extent of work, installment terms, cutoff times, and administration assumptions.

Rent Arrangements: For organizations leasing or renting property, rent arrangements lay out the details of the rent, including rent, length, and obligations of both the landowner and inhabitant.

Terms of Administration (ToS) and Protection Strategies: Online organizations frequently require ToS and security arrangements to educate clients regarding their limitations while utilizing a site or application. These strategies assist organizations with following legitimate prerequisites connected with client information and online exchanges.

Successful agreement drafting is a particular expertise that requires clearness, accuracy, and a profound comprehension of legitimate terms and ideas. It is prudent to look for legitimate advice while making or assessing agreements to guarantee that they are lawfully strong and defensive of your inclinations. Appropriately executed agreements can forestall questions and give a legitimate structure to tending to conflicts or breaks.

Chapter 4

The Execution Phase

The execution stage is a basic part of any task or try, filling in as the extension among arranging and acknowledgment. It is the stage where all the fastidious preparation, asset portion, and planning come full circle in unmistakable activities and results. Whether with regards to a business project, a tactical mission, a development try, or some other complex endeavor, the execution stage is where everything becomes real, where hypotheses and thoughts are scrutinized, and where the achievement or disappointment of the whole not set in stone.

In this rambling account, we will dig profound into the complexities of the execution stage, investigating its importance, difficulties, and key standards. We will travel through different areas, from business and innovation to workmanship and science, to uncover the ongoing ideas that wind through effective executions. This story isn't simply a specialized manual or an administration guide; it is a complete investigation of human undertaking and how the execution progressively ease assumes a critical part in molding our reality.

The execution stage isn't only the demonstration of doing; a powerful interaction requires a mix of arranging, variation, initiative, and the aggregate endeavors of people. It is the second when goals are changed over into activities, and methodologies are changed into results. A top notch plan resembles an ensemble showing some signs of life, where each instrument adds to the concordance of the entire, and any stumble can disturb the whole organization.

In the realm of business, execution is in many cases hailed as the differentiator between effective organizations and their less lucky partners. Numerous thoughts and systems might be visionary, however their execution isolates them from simple dreams. A perfect representation is the tale of Apple Inc., which has reliably shown the force of execution in transforming imaginative ideas into the real world. The organization's set of experiences is a demonstration of its capacity to bring extraordinary innovations, like the iPhone and iPad, to showcase with exceptional accuracy and achievement.

The execution stage is additionally vital in military tasks. In the confusion of mass conflict, where designs frequently slam into the unusual real factors of the front line, execution turns into an immeasurably significant issue. Fruitful military execution requires a harmony among adaptability and discipline, with leaders settling on constant choices in view of the developing circumstance. The Skirmish of Stalingrad during The Second Great War is a perfect representation of how successful execution, joined with versatility, can change the direction of history. The Soviet safeguards of the city, drove by Broad Georgy Zhukov, exhibited phenomenal strength and versatility, eventually crushing the German powers through their sheer capacity to execute and adjust under desperate conditions.

In addition, the execution stage is fundamental in the domain of development and designing activities. From building the pyramids of Egypt to developing current high rises, the capacity to execute mind boggling plans is essential. These undertakings depend on exact coordination, asset the board, and talented work to guarantee that the fabulous plans imagined by designers and architects become strong designs that endure for the long haul. The development of the Burj Khalifa in Dubai, as of now the tallest structure on the planet, represents how execution greatness can prompt earth shattering accomplishments. The venture's prosperity was a consequence of careful preparation and a tireless spotlight on execution, beating various specialized difficulties and strategic obstacles.

In logical pursuits, execution assumes a vital part in carrying momentous revelations to completion. Researchers frequently go through years creating theories, planning analyses, and gathering information. Notwithstanding, it is the execution of these tests and the thorough investigation of information that lead to logical forward leaps. The well known illustration of the Huge Hadron Collider at CERN, which prompted the disclosure of the Higgs boson, features the significance of execution in exploratory material science. The collider, a huge and complex machine, expected flawless execution at each level to accomplish its logical objectives.

Creative undertakings are no special case for the meaning of the execution stage. Painters, journalists, artists, and entertainers should rejuvenate their innovative dreams through capable execution. In the realm of writing, the fastidious execution of composing, altering, and distributing can change a writer's thoughts into a top of the line novel. Crafted by prestigious creators like J.K. Rowling and George R.R. Martin are perfect representations of how execution can spellbind and captivate perusers.

The domain of innovation is another field where execution has a significant effect. Mechanical developments, from the making of the Internet to the improvement of cell phones, are a demonstration of the force of execution. Tim Berners-Lee's execution of his vision for a worldwide data framework changed the world, while organizations like Apple and Google have reliably shown the ability of execution in carrying state of the art innovations to the majority.

The way to fruitful execution is loaded with difficulties, and understanding these difficulties is significant for anybody trying to accomplish their objectives. One of the main difficulties is the requirement for powerful initiative. The execution stage requires pioneers who can motivate and direct groups, pursue basic choices under tension, and adjust to unexpected conditions. Pioneers should be visionaries, planners, and inspirations, fit for joining different gifts toward a shared objective. They should likewise be ready to get a sense of ownership with the two victories and disappointments, as execution is a common undertaking with individual responsibility.

Besides, asset the board is a vital test in execution. Whether regarding time, cash, materials, or HR, compelling allotment and use are essential. Bungle of assets can prompt deferrals, cost invades, and shoddy outcomes. Organizations like Toyota have succeeded in this viewpoint by carrying out the Toyota Creation Framework, a creation reasoning that spotlights on limiting waste and enhancing asset usage. The outcome is an exceptionally productive and responsive execution process.

Another critical test is risk the executives. The execution stage is intrinsically hazardous, as it includes transforming plans into reality in a dynamic and frequently capricious climate. Perceiving likely dangers and creating emergency courses of action is fundamental. The aeronautic trade, for example, is known for its thorough gamble the executives in the execution of room missions. Space travelers and specialists are prepared to oversee risk and answer surprising difficulties in the unforgiving climate of room.

Correspondence is one more test in execution. Successful correspondence guarantees that all colleagues are lined up with the venture's objectives, figure out their jobs, and can adjust to evolving conditions. Miscommunication can prompt disarray, clashes, and, at last, project disappointment. The avionics business is eminent for its accentuation on clear correspondence conventions, which are fundamental for the wellbeing and effective execution of flights.

Versatility is an essential component in the execution stage, especially in quickly evolving conditions. Plans might should be changed on the fly to answer surprising turns of events or make the most of new open doors. The progress of Netflix in changing from a DVD rental support of a streaming goliath is a great representation of how flexibility in execution can prompt surprising results. Netflix's leaders perceived the moving scene of diversion and executed an essential turn that reformed the business.

An ongoing idea in the execution stage is the requirement for accuracy. The unseen details are the main problem, and, surprisingly, a little oversight can have huge results. Whether in assembling, medical services, or money, accuracy is fundamental. The medical services area, for instance, depends on the accuracy execution of operations, findings, and therapy plans. Mistakes can prompt patient damage, making accuracy a non-debatable component of execution.

The computerized age has acquainted another aspect with execution with the approach of undertaking the board and joint effort devices. These devices give a stage to arranging, correspondence, and undertaking the board, smoothing out the execution interaction. Stages like Asana, Trello, and Slack have altered how groups coordinate their endeavors, empowering ongoing joint effort and progress following.

Notwithstanding project the executives apparatuses, information examination and man-made consciousness (computer based intelligence) are progressively molding the execution stage. Information driven direction and prescient examination assist associations with advancing their execution procedures. Artificial intelligence, then again, is being utilized in businesses like medical care to improve the accuracy and proficiency of surgeries and conclusion.

Coordinated effort and cooperation are at the core of fruitful execution. In the present interconnected world, groups frequently length geographic limits, cooperating from assorted areas. Virtual groups are a demonstration of the significance of successful coordinated effort instruments and systems. The Coronavirus pandemic, which constrained numerous associations to take on remote work, sped up the utilization of virtual coordinated effort stages like Zoom and Microsoft Groups. The capacity to facilitate and execute projects with a conveyed labor force is currently a basic expertise for some associations.

It's critical to perceive that execution is definitely not a direct interaction; it is iterative. In complex activities, changes and refinements are much of the time vital as new data opens up or as conditions change. The idea of the "Deft" procedure in programming advancement, for example, exemplifies this thought of iterative execution.

4.1. Overcoming challenges and setbacks

Defeating difficulties and misfortunes is an intrinsic piece of the human experience. It's the craft of exploring through snags, difficulty, and disappointments, arising on the opposite side more grounded and stronger. This excursion is all inclusive, rising above age, culture, and foundation. Whether in private undertakings, proficient yearnings, or more extensive life objectives, we as a whole face difficulties and mishaps at different places in our lives. This account investigates the meaning of conquering difficulties and misfortunes, the different structures they can take, and the techniques that can be utilized to win over them.

Difficulties and mishaps manifest in endless structures. They can be private, for example, confronting medical problems, wrestling with misfortune, or managing relationship issues. On an expert level, difficulties might emerge as monetary mishaps, vocation snags, or work environment clashes. Cultural difficulties, as monetary slumps, cataclysmic events, or worldwide emergencies, likewise influence people and networks. Difficulties can go from the unremarkable and routine to the exceptional and life changing, and they frequently test the restrictions of one's strength and assurance.

Conquering difficulties and misfortunes isn't just about overcoming snags yet in addition about self-improvement and change. When confronted with misfortune, people are constrained to adjust, foster new abilities, and gain a more profound comprehension of themselves and their general surroundings. In numerous ways, the excursion through challenges molds character, encourages shrewdness, and develops internal fortitude.

Quite possibly of the most widely recognized and general test individuals face is that of individual misfortune. Pain, in the entirety of its structures, is a huge piece of the human experience. Losing a friend or family member is perhaps of the most significant test one can experience. The lamenting system is seriously private, and it tends to be a long and twisting street toward recuperation. Individuals who have lost relatives or dear companions frequently discuss the profound distress and personal commotion that goes with such a misfortune. Nonetheless, numerous people ultimately figure out how to recuperate, drawing on their internal strength and backing from others to explore the difficult way of melancholy.

In the expert circle, profession mishaps are a typical event. Whether it's horrible a task, confronting stagnation in one's vocation, or managing work environment clashes, these difficulties can genuinely burden. The sensation of dismissal, disillusionment, and monetary flimsiness that frequently goes with these misfortunes can overpower. By the by, vocation difficulties are likewise open doors for development and redirection. Numerous effective people have confirmed that they accomplished their most noteworthy achievements subsequent to encountering critical profession misfortunes. For example, Steve Occupations was terminated from Mac, the organization he helped to establish, just to return later and lead it to significantly more noteworthy levels.

Monetary difficulties are one more typical type of affliction. Financial slumps, individual obligation, and surprising costs can all make huge obstacles. Monetary misfortunes can prompt sensations of vulnerability, tension, and despondency. Be that as it may, they can likewise act as defining moments for people to reconsider their monetary propensities, look for help, and foster more strong monetary preparation. The tale of Warren Buffett, who transformed a humble interest into a huge fortune, is a demonstration of how monetary difficulties can be changed into potential open doors with the right outlook and approach.

Wellbeing related difficulties, including physical and emotional well-being issues, can especially request. Adapting to a sickness, injury, or ongoing condition can be genuinely, inwardly, and monetarily depleting. It requires clinical treatment as well as mental strength and an emotionally supportive network of friends and family. Numerous people who have confronted wellbeing challenges have arisen with a newly discovered appreciation forever and a pledge to caring more for themselves.

Relationship challenges, be they inside families, fellowships, or heartfelt associations, can likewise be profoundly difficult. Clashes, errors, and separations can bring profound close to home agony and disturbance. Nonetheless, fruitful route of these difficulties frequently brings about more grounded, stronger connections. Individuals who have encountered rough fixes in their connections have the chance to become together, further develop correspondence, and extend their associations.

Cultural difficulties, like catastrophic events and financial emergencies, influence whole networks and even countries. These difficulties test the aggregate versatility and fortitude of a general public. Even with such affliction, networks frequently meet up, offering backing, help, and assets to help those generally impacted. Tropical storm Katrina in 2005, for instance, was a staggering catastrophic event, yet it likewise displayed the strength of the impacted networks and the commitment of people on call and volunteers who came to their guide.

As the world turns out to be progressively interconnected, worldwide difficulties, similar to the Coronavirus pandemic, highlight the significance of global joint effort and a planned reaction. The pandemic impacted essentially every side of the globe, uncovering the association of countries and the requirement for aggregate activity. The turn of events and circulation of immunizations against the infection, in record time, represent the potential for human resourcefulness and worldwide collaboration in beating even the most overwhelming difficulties.

It's vital to perceive that mishaps and difficulties are not innately negative. They are essential for the excursion, and they frequently catalyze individual and aggregate development. The Japanese specialty of Kintsugi, the act of fixing broken earthenware with gold or silver polish, is a wonderful illustration for this idea. Rather than stowing away or disposing of broken pieces, Kintsugi features the breaks and blemishes, making the piece significantly more important. Likewise, people can rise up out of difficulties and misfortunes with an extraordinary marvel, strength, and versatility that was fashioned in the cauldron of difficulty.

Defeating difficulties and misfortunes is certainly not a one-size-fits-all interaction. It changes from one individual to another and relies upon the idea of the test. Notwithstanding, there are some general systems that can assist people and networks with exploring misfortune actually:

Strength: It is fundamental to Foster versatility. Strength is the capacity to return from mishaps and difficulties. It includes a blend of mental strength, versatility, and a development outlook. Individuals with elevated degrees of versatility are better prepared to deal with affliction and push ahead.

Looking for Help: It's vital to rest on an emotionally supportive network of companions, family, and experts. Sharing one's difficulties and looking for counsel or basically a listening ear can give close to home help and commonsense direction. Support gatherings and directing can be important assets for those confronting huge difficulties.

Self-Reflection: Misfortunes frequently give an open door to self-reflection. What can be gained from the experience? How might it prompt self-awareness or a shift in course? Self-reflection can assist people with tracking down importance and reason in their difficulties.

Care and Stress Decrease: Care rehearses, like reflection and profound breathing activities, can assist with lessening pressure and tension. These practices advance a feeling of quiet and clearness, permitting people to all the more likely explore their difficulties.

Laying out Little Objectives: While confronting significant misfortunes, it tends to be useful to separate the recuperation interaction into more modest, sensible advances. Defining little objectives and accomplishing them can fabricate a feeling of achievement and inspiration.

Looking for Proficient Assistance: For challenges connected with psychological wellness, looking for the help of a specialist, instructor, or therapist can be pivotal. Emotional well-being experts can give significant direction and backing.

Acquiring and Ability Advancement: A few difficulties might require the improvement of new abilities or information. Taking courses, looking for mentorship, or getting to assets can upgrade one's capacity to defeat difficulties.

Keeping an Inspirational perspective: Keeping an inspirational perspective doesn't mean overlooking the earnestness of difficulties. It implies developing idealism, trust, and a confidence in one's capacity to conquer difficulty. An uplifting perspective can be a strong driver of flexibility.

Local area and Social Commitment: Drawing in with one's local area or partaking in charitable effort can give a feeling of motivation and association. Helping other people can be a method for mending and track down importance in testing times.

Time and Tolerance: Defeating critical difficulties frequently takes time. It's vital to show restraint toward oneself and comprehend that recuperating and recuperation are slow cycles.

The narratives of people who have defeated monstrous difficulties and misfortunes act as a demonstration of the versatility of the human soul. The existence of Helen Keller, for example, represents the force of assurance and persistence. Notwithstanding being both visually impaired and hard of hearing since early on, she proceeded to turn into a prestigious creator, teacher, and promoter for individuals with incapacities. Her process was not without its portion of deterrents, but rather her unflinching soul and persistent quest for information permitted her to win over affliction.

The idea of post-horrible development is one more component of defeating difficulties. It proposes that people who have encountered critical injury or misfortune can encounter self-awareness and change therefore. Instead of being for all time scarred by their encounters, they arise with a recharged feeling of direction, a more profound appreciation forever, and a more noteworthy comprehension of their own versatility. The narrative of Malala Yousafzai, the Pakistani instruction lobbyist who endure a death endeavor by the Taliban, embodies this idea.

4.2. Navigating the complexities of the market

Exploring the intricacies of the market is an imposing errand, whether with regards to business, money, or even private ventures. The market, as a dynamic and frequently erratic substance, is impacted by a large number of variables, including monetary circumstances, innovative headways, customer conduct, and international occasions.

Effectively exploring the market requires a sharp comprehension of its complexities, a strong technique, and the capacity to adjust to evolving conditions. In this story, we will dive profound into the intricacies of the market, investigating the key rules that support it, the difficulties it presents, and the procedures that can be utilized to get by as well as flourish inside its dynamic scene.

At the center of understanding business sector intricacies lies the idea of market interest. This essential monetary guideline frames the establishment whereupon markets work. Generally, the cost of an item or still up in the air by the harmony between supply, the amount accessible, and request, the craving for that item or administration. At the point when request surpasses supply, costs will quite often rise, and when supply outperforms request, costs ordinarily fall. It's a fragile dance among purchasers and makers, and it's the main impetus behind cost changes in different business sectors.

Worldwide business sectors, whether for merchandise, administrations, or monetary instruments, are impacted by a plenty of interconnected factors. Financial circumstances assume a significant part in market elements. Factors like expansion, joblessness, and loan costs significantly affect the way of behaving of purchasers, organizations, and financial backers. A powerful economy frequently prompts expanded shopper spending and business speculation, while a drowsy economy can bring about diminished spending and venture, causing far reaching influences all through the market.

Mechanical headways and advancement are impetuses for market development. The fast speed of innovative change has upset conventional ventures and set out new open doors. Organizations like Apple and Amazon have reshaped purchaser conduct and whole market scenes through imaginative items and administrations. The people who adjust to mechanical headways and expect their suggestions are in many cases better situated to flourish on the lookout.

Purchaser conduct, driven by social movements, patterns, and inclinations, impacts markets. Socioeconomics, like generational contrasts, can shape market interest and patterns. For instance, the millennial age's inclination for internet shopping and advanced administrations has driven web based business and fintech developments.

International occasions, from exchange wars and clashes to worldwide wellbeing emergencies, can possibly annoy markets. These occasions present vulnerability, which can prompt market instability. The Coronavirus pandemic, for example, disturbed worldwide stockpile chains as well as changed shopper conduct, with extensive ramifications for businesses like travel, amusement, and retail.

Monetary business sectors, including stocks, securities, and monetary forms, are affected by different variables, including financing costs, money related approach, and financial backer feeling. The choices made by national banks, like the Central bank in the US or the European National Bank, can essentially affect market liquidity and getting costs. The feeling of financial backers, impacted by news, political occasions, and monetary information, can drive market changes.

Housing markets, both private and business, are dependent upon exceptional elements. Factors like area, populace development, and lodging supply can influence property estimations. The 2008 worldwide monetary emergency, brought about by a real estate market breakdown in the US, showed how interconnected land is with monetary business sectors and the more extensive economy.

Item advertises, which include unrefined components like oil, gold, and horticultural items, are impacted by organic market, as well as international occasions. Product costs are especially delicate to factors like weather patterns, economic deals, and international unsteadiness. The change of oil costs, frequently determined by political pressures in oil-creating areas, highlights the worldwide effect of item advertises.

Exploring the intricacies of the market requires a strong comprehension of hazard. All types of speculation accompany a degree of chance, and the potential for the two increases and misfortunes. Risk the executives is a basic expertise for financial backers and organizations.

Enhancement, or spreading speculations across various resource classes, is a typical methodology to relieve risk. Expansion safeguards against critical misfortunes in a solitary resource or market.

Risk evaluation, frequently utilizing devices like gamble reward examination or situation arranging, is a urgent piece of venture choices. Financial backers and organizations should think about the likely disadvantage of a speculation or market choice and weigh it against the normal return.

For people exploring the intricacies of the market, monetary proficiency is central. Understanding ideas like planning, saving, and contributing is vital for pursuing informed monetary choices. Numerous people depend on venture vehicles like retirement accounts, for example, 401(k)s, to create long haul financial wellbeing. A broadened arrangement of stocks, bonds, and different resources is frequently prescribed to spread risk and accomplish long haul monetary objectives.

In the realm of business venture and business, market intricacies are a steady test. New companies frequently face extreme contest, financing difficulties, and market vacillations. It's significant for business people to lead exhaustive statistical surveying, recognize one of a kind incentives, and adjust to changing economic situations. Fruitful business visionaries frequently have a blend of development, flexibility, and a capacity to turn when important.

For laid out organizations, market intricacies require continuous vital preparation. Business pioneers should expect changes in buyer conduct, mechanical headways, and financial circumstances. Organizations like IBM, which progressed from equipment assembling to programming and administrations, have exhibited the significance of adjusting to advancing business sectors.

Monetary business sectors present an extraordinary arrangement of intricacies. The financial exchange, specifically, is described by its day to day cost vacillations and is impacted by a huge number of elements, including organization execution, monetary circumstances, and financial backer opinion. Fruitful financial backers frequently utilize techniques, for example, key investigation, which assesses an organization's monetary wellbeing, and specialized examination, which surveys verifiable value patterns and examples.

Financial backers likewise should settle on long haul and momentary venture procedures. Long haul financial backers frequently center around building a differentiated arrangement of resources fully intent on holding them for a considerable length of time or even many years. Momentary financial backers, then again, as often as possible take part in exchanging, endeavoring to benefit from cost changes throughout more limited time spans.

Risk resilience is a vital thought for financial backers. A few financial backers are risk-opposed and focus on resource safeguarding. They might choose more moderate ventures, for example, securities or profit yielding stocks. Others are risk-open minded and will acknowledge more elevated levels of chance for the capability of more noteworthy returns. The gamble return compromise is a basic idea in finance, which recommends that more significant yields normally accompany more serious gamble.

The significance of morals and mindful putting has acquired unmistakable quality lately. Numerous financial backers focus on ecological, social, and administration (ESG) rules while settling on speculation choices. ESG contributing thinks about monetary returns as well as the effect of ventures on society and the climate. Organizations that display dependable strategic policies and manageability frequently line up with the upsides of ESG-centered financial backers.

In the domain of exchanging, high-recurrence exchanging (HFT) is a training that depends on cutting edge calculations and PC frameworks to execute huge number of exchanges inside milliseconds. HFT enjoys carried the two benefits and worries to monetary business sectors. On one hand, it has further developed market liquidity and diminished bid-ask spreads. Then again, it has brought up issues about market solidness and decency, as HFT frameworks can set off fast and frequently eccentric cost swings.

Monetary business sectors are likewise affected by financial arrangement, which includes choices made by national banks with respect to loan fees and cash supply. For example, the Central bank's choice to bring down financing costs can invigorate acquiring and burning through, possibly supporting monetary development. Alternately, raising financing costs can assist with controling expansion however may slow monetary movement.

4.3. The role of resilience and adaptability

The job of flexibility and versatility in the human experience couldn't possibly be more significant. These characteristics are fundamental to explore the horde difficulties and misfortunes that life tosses our direction, to flourish in steadily evolving conditions, and to outfit open doors for individual and aggregate development. In this account, we will dive profound into the meaning of strength and versatility, investigating their major standards, their part in confronting affliction, and the systems that can be utilized to develop and use these characteristics to conquer impediments and thrive in an always advancing world.

Versatility, at its center, is the ability to return quickly from difficulty, to get through difficulty, and to recuperate from misfortunes. A mental and close to home strength empowers people to endure pressure and tension, to persist despite difficulties, and to rise up out of troublesome conditions with freshly discovered intelligence and courage. Flexibility is definitely not a static characteristic; a powerful quality can be created and sharpened over the long run.

Flexibility, then again, is the capacity to acclimate to new circumstances and evolving conditions. It incorporates adaptability, genius, and the ability to embrace change. Versatility is a crucial expertise in a world set apart by consistent motion, development, and vulnerability. It permits people to answer successfully to moving conditions, immediately jump all over new chances, and diagram a course through unknown region.

The significance of flexibility and versatility becomes obvious when we look at the many difficulties and mishaps that people face in their own lives. Individual affliction can take on different structures, including medical conditions, relationship hardships, monetary difficulties, and individual misfortune. Every one of these difficulties requests a remarkable sort of versatility and flexibility.

In the domain of wellbeing, flexibility assumes a critical part in confronting sickness, injury, or constant circumstances. People who show versatility frequently adapt all the more really to wellbeing related difficulties. They show an uplifting perspective, keep a battling soul, and effectively take part in their treatment and recuperation. Versatility can likewise be a wellspring of help for relatives and parental figures who explore the profound and reasonable intricacies of medical care.

Pain and misfortune are essential pieces of the human experience. The departure of a friend or family member can be a significant personal test, requesting a huge measure of flexibility to persevere through the torment and to push ahead. The individuals who have encountered misfortune frequently go through a complex lamenting cycle, set apart by phases of disavowal, outrage, dealing, misery, and acknowledgment. The versatility expected to explore this cycle is a demonstration of the human soul's striking limit with respect to recuperating and reestablishment.

Relationship challenges, whether in familial, heartfelt, or companionship settings, are another region where flexibility and versatility are vital. Correspondence breakdowns, clashes, and the conclusion of friendships can genuinely burden. Strength in these circumstances includes a readiness to face issues, look for goal, and develop from the experience. Versatility, then again, is the ability to conform to changing elements in connections and to perceive when the time has come to relinquish unfortunate associations.

Monetary difficulties, including employment misfortune, obligation, or financial slumps, represent a particular arrangement of difficulties. Versatility notwithstanding monetary difficulty is set apart by genius, planning, and tracking down new open doors. People who have confronted monetary difficulty frequently find an inward strength and assurance to modify their monetary soundness. Flexibility in this setting implies being available to new vocation ways, gaining new abilities, and embracing monetary procedures that line up with evolving conditions.

Individual difficulties can likewise incorporate conquering fixation, overseeing psychological wellness issues, and finding one's motivation and energy. These excursions request elevated degrees of flexibility, as people defy their weaknesses and work towards personal development. Versatility is the main thrust behind recuperation and the excursion toward mental and profound prosperity.

Additionally, the flexibility to evolving conditions, including the effect of new advances and moving financial scenes, is fundamental in proficient undertakings. The contemporary workplace is set apart by a determined speed of progress. Computerization and man-made reasoning have changed enterprises, reshaping position jobs and setting out new open doors. The Coronavirus pandemic, with its far reaching reception of remote work, highlighted the significance of flexibility as associations explored startling difficulties.

Versatility in the expert setting is the ability to endure vocation misfortunes, for example, employment misfortune or work environment clashes, without failing to focus on one's expert objectives. It includes keeping up with inspiration and fearlessness notwithstanding difficulty. For instance, fruitful business people frequently trait their accomplishments to their capacity to gain from disappointments and adjust their business systems as needs be.

Flexibility in the expert domain is the capacity to obtain new abilities, embrace mechanical changes, and turn in light of market shifts. Exemplified by people constantly update their ranges of abilities to stay cutthroat in the gig market. Long lasting learning, worked with by online courses and instructive assets, is a useful sign of versatility in the present proficient world.

Moreover, flexibility and versatility are not restricted to the person. They are additionally urgent characteristics in viable administration. Pioneers should direct their associations through changing economic situations, monetary choppiness, and industry interruptions. The Coronavirus pandemic tried the initiative of organizations and legislatures around the world. Pioneers who exhibited versatility and flexibility successfully directed their groups through the emergency.

4.4. The iterative process and lessons learned

The iterative interaction is a crucial idea that supports human advancement and advancement across different spaces, from business and innovation to self-improvement and imaginative pursuits. It addresses a repetitive way to deal with critical thinking and improvement, wherein errands and tasks are returned to and refined through rehashed patterns of assessment and change. This iterative methodology is an amazing asset for learning, variation, and development, and it permits people and associations to tweak their techniques and accomplish improved results after some time. In this account, we will investigate the meaning of the iterative cycle, its application in various settings, and the important examples that can be learned through this ceaseless pattern of refinement.

The iterative cycle is profoundly implanted in the texture of human undertaking. At its center, it typifies that the way to progress is seldom direct or clear; rather, it includes a progression of input circles, each structure upon the last, to accomplish improved results. This idea is particularly articulated in the area of innovation, where iterative advancement has upset how programming is made.

In programming improvement, the lithe approach embodies the force of emphasis. Light-footed standards advance adaptability, cooperation, and responsiveness to change, permitting improvement groups to deliver continuous, little updates to their product. This iterative methodology urges groups to work in short cycles or "runs," commonly enduring half a month, during which they configuration, construct, test, and refine their product. These emphasess empower the fast fuse of client criticism, ID of issues, and transformation to evolving prerequisites. Nimble improvement has turned into the business standard for building top notch programming and has cultivated a culture of consistent improvement.

The iterative interaction isn't bound to the universe of innovation. It is similarly significant in different ventures, from item plan and assembling to project the executives and medical care. The idea of persistent improvement, as typified by the Toyota Creation Framework, is a deep rooted illustration of the iterative cycle in assembling. Toyota's methodology underscores the end of waste, further developed proficiency, and a guarantee to consistent refinement. The iterative outlook, frequently called "kaizen," is tied in with making little, gradual enhancements that gather over the long haul to yield significant advantages.

Project the executives is another area where the iterative cycle is fundamental. The task the executives approach known as "Scrum" applies iterative standards to convey complex undertakings. Scrum separates the task into a progression of emphasess, called "runs," which ordinarily last two to about a month. Toward the finish of each run, the group surveys what has been achieved, distinguishes difficulties, and changes their arrangement for the following run. This iterative methodology permits groups to answer developing undertaking necessities, lessen risk, and keep an emphasis on conveying esteem.

In medical services, the iterative cycle is vital to working on understanding consideration and clinical therapies. Clinical preliminaries, for example, frequently go through different stages, with each stage expanding upon the information acquired from the past one. The iterative idea of clinical preliminaries guarantees that medicines and mediations are thoroughly tried, refined, and improved before they are acquainted with a more extensive patient populace. This interaction is indispensable for patient security and the improvement of compelling clinical intercessions.

The iterative interaction isn't exclusively a hierarchical or proficient idea; it is similarly material to self-improvement. People endeavoring to accomplish individual objectives, whether in wellbeing and wellness, training, or imaginative pursuits, should explore their own iterative process. This individual excursion frequently includes setting clear targets, making a move, pondering headway, and making changes in view of what has been realized.

One of the huge difficulties in self-improvement is keeping up with inspiration and discipline over the long haul. Many individuals put forth objectives yet battle to reliably execute them. This is where the iterative interaction assumes a significant part. It urges people to break their objectives into more modest, feasible errands and to return to and refine their methodologies as they progress. It advances a feeling of flexibility and a comprehension that difficulties and misfortunes are a characteristic piece of the excursion.

The iterative cycle in self-improvement is firmly connected with the idea of propensity arrangement and self-control. Constructing and supporting propensities that help the ideal objectives is a fundamental piece of self-improvement. The reiteration of positive ways of behaving and the disposal of negative ones through iterative cycles lead to enduring change. Writer James Clear, in his book "Nuclear Propensities," accentuates the force of little, predictable changes in building propensities that can prompt amazing changes over the long run.

Besides, the possibility of flexibility assumes a huge part in self-improvement inside the iterative cycle. Life frequently tosses unforeseen difficulties and misfortunes, and strength is the capacity to quickly return from affliction and proceed with the execution of one's objectives. Individual flexibility is a quality frequently connected with people who have made wonderful progress notwithstanding difficulty. The iterative cycle permits people to draw on their flexibility, adjust their techniques, and endure despite difficulties.

One of the basic illustrations that the iterative cycle confers is the worth of disappointment as a wellspring of learning and development. Disappointment is in many cases seen as an adverse result, however inside the iterative structure, it turns into a necessary piece of the criticism circle. Each time an arrangement or venture misses the mark concerning assumptions, there is a chance to inspect what turned out badly, recognize regions for development, and make the fundamental changes for the following cycle.

Thomas Edison's well known expression about concocting the light epitomizes this viewpoint: "I have not fizzled. I've quite recently found 10,000 different ways that won't work." Edison's iterative way to deal with development prompted the possible outcome of the light. He saw every disappointment as a stage toward the possible arrangement. This outlook is a basic illustration from the iterative cycle: disappointment isn't the end yet a venturing stone on the way to progress.

Disappointment, when drawn closer with flexibility and versatility, gives important experiences. It prompts people and groups to pose basic inquiries: What caused the disappointment? What can be gained from it? How might the methodology be changed in accordance with stay away from comparable entanglements later on? The iterative cycle empowers a culture of constant learning and development through the acknowledgment that misfortunes are an inborn piece of the excursion to progress.

Besides, the iterative interaction underscores the significance of input. Criticism, whether from clients, partners, or individual reflection, is an important wellspring of data that can illuminate upgrades. In the realm of business and item advancement, criticism from clients and clients is fundamental. Organizations like Apple and Amazon have flourished by effectively looking for and integrating client input into their item advancement processes. The iterative pattern of delivery, assemble input, change, and delivery again is a demonstrated technique for making items that reverberate with clients.

In project the executives, the iterative cycle permits groups to distinguish issues and make course revisions right off the bat in the task, lessening the probability of exorbitant deferrals or disappointments. This proactive way to deal with project the executives lines up with the rule that distinguishing and resolving issues as soon as possible is more proficient and compelling.

In self-improvement, self-reflection and criticism from guides, mentors, or friends can be instrumental in distinguishing regions for development. The method involved with laying out objectives, making a move, considering progress, and changing the methodology in view of criticism permits people to refine their systems and advance toward their goals persistently.

The iterative cycle additionally features the meaning of flexibility. In a quickly impacting world, people and associations that are impervious to change are in a difficult situation. Versatility is the ability to embrace change, whether driven by outside factors or the acknowledgment of chances for development. It is tied in with being available to new data, changing one's methodology, and developing with the evolving scene.

The Coronavirus pandemic, for instance, constrained associations and people to adjust to remote work, travel limitations, and new wellbeing and security conventions. The people who adjusted rapidly to the new truths were better situated to climate the emergency. Flexibility is a quality that empowers people and associations to flourish even with vulnerability and disturbance.

Additionally, the iterative interaction stresses the significance of laying out clear and quantifiable objectives. Objectives give guidance and motivation, directing people and associations in their endeavors. The iterative methodology includes separating these general objectives into more modest, reasonable errands or achievements. These more modest objectives are more feasible and give a feeling of progress and achievement, which can persuade.

The idea of Brilliant objectives — objectives that are Explicit, Quantifiable, Feasible, Pertinent, and Time-bound — is frequently used to make successful targets. This system urges people to characterize their objectives with accuracy, recognize how they will quantify achievement, guarantee that the objectives are sensible, pertinent to their bigger points, and set cutoff times for finish.

Chapter 5

Pivoting and Adapting

Turning and adjusting are two fundamental techniques in the steadily advancing scene of business, advancement, and self-improvement. In a world set apart by quick change, unanticipated difficulties, and surprising open doors, the capacity to turn and adjust is in many cases the distinction among progress and stagnation. Whether with regards to business venture, mechanical development, or self-awareness, the ability to change course, change techniques, and embrace new points of view is a basic expertise that can prompt wonderful results. In this story, we will investigate the meaning of turning and adjusting, looking at their applications in different spaces and the important examples they bestow.

The Specialty of Turning:

Turning is an idea frequently connected with business and new companies. It alludes to an essential change in a plan of action, item, or target market to answer changing conditions or to find a superior item market fit. The capacity to turn is basic for beginning phase organizations, as it permits them to explore vulnerability, refine their incentive, and at last increment their odds of coming out on top.

One of the most notable instances of a fruitful turn in the startup world is that of Twitter. At first, Twitter was a digital recording stage called Odeo. Be that as it may, when Apple declared the send off of iTunes with webcast support, Odeo confronted outdated nature. The organization's pioneers chose to turn and investigate new open doors. This prompted the formation of Twitter, a microblogging stage, which turned into a worldwide peculiarity.

Turning can take different structures. It can include changing an item's highlights, changing evaluating systems, focusing on an alternate client section, or in any event, entering totally new business sectors. The key is to stay adaptable and open to new bearings while remaining lined up with the organization's center mission and values.

In the realm of laid out organizations, turning isn't just a system for new businesses; it's a method for remaining serious and pertinent. For instance, Adobe, an organization at first known for its product items like Photoshop and Artist, turned to a membership based model with Adobe Imaginative Cloud. This essential shift permitted the organization to adjust to changing client inclinations and remain at the cutting edge of the imaginative programming industry.

Turning is additionally applicable with regards to mechanical development. Numerous weighty revelations and creations have happened because of analysts and trailblazers turning from their unique objectives. For example, the Post-it Note, presently an omnipresent office supply, was the consequence of a turn by a researcher at 3M who was attempting to foster a super-solid cement.

The capacity to turn isn't restricted to the business world. It is similarly crucial in self-awareness. People frequently put forth objectives and set out on ways that they later find are not lined up with their qualities, interests, or evolving conditions. In such cases, turning can include making a huge profession change, modifying way of life decisions, or rethinking individual objectives.

One of the difficulties in self-awareness is perceiving when the time has come to turn. It might include a time of self-reflection, looking for direction from guides or mentors, and assessing whether the ongoing way is prompting the ideal results. Turning can be a gallant step, as it frequently requires relinquishing the natural and embracing the unexplored world.

The most common way of turning is firmly connected with flexibility. Flexibility is the capacity to conform to new circumstances and evolving conditions. A quality permits people and associations to embrace change, answer really to difficulties, and quickly jump all over chances.

The Force of Transformation:

Transformation is a crucial idea in science, where it portrays how species develop to make due and flourish in evolving conditions. Charles Darwin's hypothesis of development by regular determination features that creatures that adjust to their environmental elements are bound to give their qualities to the future.

This standard of transformation isn't restricted to science; it applies to numerous parts of human existence. With regards to self-awareness, transformation is the ability to transform one's way of behaving, systems, or outlook to more readily line up with new conditions or targets. Flexibility permits people to climate mishaps, embrace new open doors, and explore the eccentric idea of life.

In business, versatility is basic for long haul achievement. Associations that stay unbending and impervious to change frequently think of themselves as abandoned. Then again, organizations that adjust to showcase shifts, purchaser inclinations, and arising advancements can remain serious and inventive.

One industry that has seen emotional change and transformation is the distributing business. With the ascent of advanced innovation, conventional distributers confronted difficulties from digital books, online substance, and independently publishing. Numerous distributers adjusted by differentiating their contributions, embracing advanced circulation, and investigating new income models. This versatility permitted them to make due and even flourish in the advanced age.

In addition, the Coronavirus pandemic highlighted the significance of versatility in different enterprises. Organizations that could rapidly turn their activities to oblige remote work, online deals, or contactless administrations were better prepared to endure the disturbance. Versatility, in this unique situation, involved changing methodologies as well as cultivating an adaptable and strong hierarchical culture.

In the domain of mechanical development, versatility is fundamental for remaining at the front line. Pioneers and creators should be available to new revelations, able to change their speculations, and ready to turn their examination in light of surprising discoveries. The historical backdrop of science and innovation is loaded with instances of versatility prompting pivotal forward leaps.

The disclosure of penicillin by Alexander Fleming is one such model. Fleming had been directing exploration on antibacterial substances and, when he got back to his lab after a get-away, found that a shape called Penicillium notatum had defiled one of his trials. He saw that the form had killed the microbes and, understanding the meaning of this opportunity revelation, turned his examination to foster penicillin, the main anti-microbial.

The idea of flexibility additionally reaches out to development inside laid out organizations. The course of open advancement, advocated by Henry Chesbrough, urges associations to be available to outer thoughts and developments. This approach perceives that not all leap forwards need to come from inside an association; they can likewise be obtained remotely through associations, acquisitions, or coordinated efforts. Being versatile and open to outside advancement can prompt extraordinary changes.

One more illustration from variation is the significance of strength. Versatility is the capacity to quickly return from affliction, mishaps, or difficulties. It includes profound mettle, a positive mentality, and an assurance to endure despite hindrances. Strength is much of the time fundamental while adjusting to new conditions, as change can be joined by vulnerability and troubles.

One of the most significant instances of flexibility and transformation is the recuperation and development of nations that have encountered critical misfortune, like conflict or financial breakdown. Germany and Japan, for example, rose up out of The Second Great War crushed at the end of the day bounced back to become monetary forces to be reckoned with through resolved endeavors and versatility.

At a singular level, versatility and transformation are significant characteristics while confronting individual difficulties or misfortunes. The capacity to adjust to unforeseen life altering situations, like the departure of a task, a wellbeing emergency, or a relationship separation, is a demonstration of individual strength. Individuals who display flexibility during such difficult times frequently attract on their versatility to investigate new open doors, change their ways of life, and track down ways of adapting and remake.

In addition, transformation likewise underlines the benefit of gaining from encounters. Whether with regards to self-improvement, business, or advancement, adjusting to new conditions frequently includes considering past activities and results. The iterative course of putting forth objectives, making a move, assessing results, and changing methodologies is a type of transformation.

Gaining as a matter of fact is an important wellspring of information. It permits people and associations to refine their methodologies, try not to rehash previous oversights, and go with informed choices. Thomas Edison, while fostering the light, broadly expressed that he had not fizzled; he had quite recently found 10,000 different ways that wouldn't work. Edison's flexibility and eagerness to gain from every "disappointment" at last prompted his innovation's prosperity.

The Advantageous Relationship:

Turning and adjusting are not totally unrelated ideas. As a matter of fact, they frequently remain closely connected, making a harmonious relationship that is strong in both self-awareness and expert undertakings. Turning frequently includes an essential change because of new data, while variation is the continuous course of embracing and flourishing in changed conditions.

Consider a business that has turned its item advertising. This essential shift might include making another item or entering an alternate market. Nonetheless, when the turn is made, the association should adjust to the new business climate. This might include refining advertising methodologies, changing stock chains, and answering client criticism. The turn starts the change, and transformation guarantees the association's continuous progress in the new heading.

5.1. Recognizing the need for change

Change is a ubiquitous power on the planet, endlessly shaping our lives, social orders, and the consistently developing scene of human undertaking. A power can be both strengthening and testing, and the capacity to perceive the requirement for change is a major impetus for self-improvement, hierarchical development, and cultural advancement. In this story, we will dig profound into the meaning of perceiving the requirement for change, investigating its applications in assorted settings, and the examples it gives.

The Certainty of Progress:

Change is a certain piece of the human experience. From the second we are conceived, our lives are described by a progression of changes. We develop actually, grow inwardly, secure information, and adjust to a consistently moving world. As we change from youth to pre-adulthood, and from adulthood to advanced age, we are ceaselessly gone up against with new conditions, jobs, and obligations.

In the more extensive setting of society, change is similarly determined. Accepted practices, social qualities, and mechanical headways advance after some time, reshaping the manner in which we live and collaborate. Financial frameworks go through vacillations, political scenes change, and logical revelations reform how we might interpret the world. The ability to perceive and answer these progressions is essential for people and associations the same.

In addition, the speed of progress has advanced in the cutting edge time. Progressions in innovation, fast globalization, and the interconnectivity of the advanced age have enhanced the speed of progress. What was viewed as historic yesterday might be obsolete tomorrow. In this unique climate, the capacity to perceive the requirement for change isn't just significant yet additionally progressively earnest.

The Individual Domain:

Perceiving the requirement for change in our own lives is a profoundly thoughtful and fundamental cycle. It includes mindfulness, reflection, and the eagerness to go up against parts of our lives that might require improvement or change. Self-awareness is a consistent excursion, and perceiving the requirement for change is the most vital move toward personal development and a satisfying life.

At the singular level, the requirement for change can appear in different ways. It very well may be the acknowledgment that a profession is done satisfying or lining up with one's interests and objectives. It very well may be a craving to further develop wellbeing and prosperity by taking on a better way of life. The requirement for change could likewise surface with regards to connections, provoking people to resolve issues, put down stopping points, or look for new associations.

One of the vital illustrations from perceiving the requirement for change in the individual domain is the significance of mindfulness. Mindfulness is the establishment whereupon self-improvement is fabricated. It includes figuring out one's assets, shortcomings, values, and yearnings. Mindfulness permits people to survey their ongoing conditions, distinguish regions for development, and decide the heading of wanted change.

Versatility and strength are likewise significant characteristics in perceiving the requirement for change in the individual domain. Change can be joined by difficulties, questions, and uneasiness. Versatility is the ability to conform to new circumstances, while strength empowers people to return quickly from misfortunes, keep an uplifting perspective, and endure through troublesome changes.

One instance of perceiving the requirement for change in self-improvement is making a lifelong shift. Many individuals wind up in vocations that, over the long run, never again satisfy them or line up with their qualities and yearnings. Perceiving the requirement for a vocation change includes recognizing that the ongoing way is at this point not the right fit and that there is potential for a seriously fulfilling and adjusted profession somewhere else.

In such cases, people frequently go through a course of self-reflection and contemplation to decide their new vocation heading. They might evaluate their abilities, interests, and values and investigate amazing open doors in various fields. This acknowledgment of the requirement for change is a valiant step, as it frequently requires abandoning the commonality of the ongoing vocation and setting out on an obscure way.

One more part of individual change is the acknowledgment of the need to embrace better propensities and ways of life. This requirement for change might emerge from wellbeing concerns, a craving to work on prosperity, or the acknowledgment that ongoing propensities are unfavorable. It involves the eagerness to defy pointless ways of behaving, like unfortunate dietary decisions, inactive ways of life, or unsafe survival techniques, and make changes toward better practices.

With regards to connections, perceiving the requirement for change can be especially difficult yet in addition groundbreaking. Connections are dynamic and advance over the long run. People might end up in connections that have become poisonous, unfulfilling, or skewed with their qualities. Perceiving the requirement for change in connections can include defining limits, looking for advising or treatment, or at last completion poisonous associations in quest for better and more steady connections.

The individual domain additionally envelops perceiving the requirement for change with regards to self-awareness and personal growth. This might include securing new abilities, chasing after schooling, or looking for self-awareness valuable chances to live up to one's true capacity. The acknowledgment that development is a continuous excursion and that there is something else to learn is a demonstration of the significance of perceiving the requirement for change at the singular level.

The Authoritative Circle:

Associations, whether organizations, charities, or government substances, are not safe to the certainty of progress. As a matter of fact, perceiving the requirement for change is in many cases a represent the deciding moment consider an association's drawn out progress. The inability to adjust and develop because of changing conditions can prompt stagnation, unimportance, or even disappointment.

In the business world, perceiving the requirement for change frequently emerges from shifts in economic situations, customer inclinations, or mechanical headways. Organizations that are delayed to perceive and answer these progressions can rapidly lose their upper hand. Then again, organizations that are capable at perceiving the requirement for change can get by as well as flourish in a powerful commercial center.

One of the most refered to instances of a business perceiving the requirement for change is the change of IBM. In the mid 1990s, IBM confronted huge monetary difficulties and an obsolete plan of action. Perceiving the requirement for change, the organization went through an extreme change. It moved its concentration from equipment to programming and administrations, embraced open guidelines, and adjusted to the changing innovation scene. This turn and variation permitted IBM to recover its situation as a worldwide forerunner in the IT business.

Another essential model is Nokia, which, when a predominant player in the cell phone market, neglected to perceive the requirement for change when the cell phone period arose. The organization's hesitance to adjust to the change in purchaser inclinations and the ascent of touch-screen cell phones prompted a decrease in its piece of the pie and a deficiency of its upper hand.

In government and policy management, perceiving the requirement for change is additionally fundamental. Cultural difficulties, monetary variances, and changes in open feeling request a responsive and versatile methodology. Legislatures that perceive the requirement for change and adjust their arrangements and administrations to resolve these issues are bound to successfully serve their constituents and keep up with public trust.

Perhaps of the most applicable model as of late is the Coronavirus pandemic. Legislatures overall were confronted with the basic to perceive the requirement for change and adjust their methodologies quickly to safeguard general wellbeing and deal with the emergency. This included carrying out lockdowns, testing and contact following, antibody appropriation, and financial upgrade measures. The acknowledgment of the requirement for change was a basic consider answering the pandemic successfully.

In philanthropic associations, perceiving the requirement for change frequently emerges from shifts in contributor needs, advancing cultural necessities, or changes in the administrative scene. Charities that are nimble and versatile can more readily satisfy their missions and stay pertinent to their objective recipients and allies.

The examples from perceiving the requirement for change in associations are diverse. They highlight the significance of versatility, an eagerness to turn, and a pledge to continuous learning and development. They likewise underscore the worth of hierarchical culture, initiative, and a proactive way to deal with change the board.

Change inside associations frequently requires solid authority that can actually impart the requirement for change, rally backing, and guide the association through advances. It likewise includes cultivating a culture that embraces change, values development, and urges representatives to contribute their experiences and thoughts for development.

Besides, perceiving the requirement for change inside associations can prompt an emphasis on manageable practices, corporate social obligation, and moral direction. It urges associations to adjust for monetary accomplishment as well as to improve society and the climate.

The Cultural Scene:

Perceiving the requirement for change isn't restricted to individual lives and associations; it stretches out to the cultural scene also. Cultural change envelops shifts in culture, values, and standards, as well as reactions to social and natural difficulties.

A huge instance of perceiving the requirement for change in the cultural domain is the worldwide development for racial and civil rights. The acknowledgment of foundational bigotry, social imbalances, and the requirement for change has prompted far and wide fights, strategy changes, and conversations about destroying.

5.2. Making critical business decisions

In the complex and steadily changing scene of business, the capacity to settle on basic choices is one of the characterizing elements of accomplishment. These choices can go from key decisions about market section to functional decisions about inventory network the executives. In this account, we will dig profound into the meaning of settling on basic business choices, investigating its applications in different settings, and the significant illustrations it confers.

The Job of Dynamic in Business:

Direction is at the center of each and every business activity, methodology, and cycle. It shapes the bearing of an organization, drives its prosperity, and impacts its upper hand. Business pioneers, from business people to Chiefs, should go with basic choices day to day. These choices can be essentially as different as setting evaluating techniques, entering new business sectors, putting resources into innovation, employing ability, or answering emergencies.

At its heart, navigation includes choosing a game-plan from among different other options. It's the most common way of picking the best way ahead in light of accessible data, examination, and judgment. In the business setting, choices can differ in scale, degree, and intricacy, yet they all significantly affect an association's presentation and main concern.

Moreover, the capacity to go with basic business choices isn't just a singular capability; an aggregate undertaking draws in whole groups and associations. Successful direction requires clear correspondence, cooperation, and arrangement among colleagues. It includes combining information, utilizing aptitude, and guaranteeing that decisions are reliable with an association's objectives and values.

The Dynamic Cycle:

Viable navigation is an organized interaction that includes a few key stages. While the cycle can be adjusted to different circumstances, the center components stay steady. These means give a structure to making educated, sane, and fruitful choices.

Recognize the Choice: The initial step is to characterize the choice that should be made. It's crucial for be clear about the issue or opportunity within reach and what the choice means to address. This stage includes grasping the specific situation, suggestions, and wanted results.

Accumulate Data: Chiefs should gather important data to illuminate their decisions. This includes directing examination, breaking down information, and looking for bits of knowledge from numerous sources. The nature of the data accumulated essentially influences the nature of the choice.

Create Choices: Think about a scope of potential choices or arrangements. Urge conceptualizing and imagination to recognize different other options. This step advances a more far reaching perspective on the circumstance and maintains a strategic distance from untimely obligation to a solitary arrangement.

Assess Choices: Evaluate every option in light of predefined measures and goals. Think about the benefits, weaknesses, dangers, and compromises related with every choice. The assessment ought to be efficient and objective.

Settle on the Choice: After cautious assessment, select the best other option. The decision ought to line up with the association's central goal, values, and targets. It might include compromises, and the chief should be ready to legitimize their decision.

Execute the Choice: Setting the choice in motion is a critical stage. It requires arranging, asset distribution, and correspondence. A first rate execution guarantees the choice's viability.

Screen and Assess: Navigation doesn't end with execution. Consistent checking and assessment are important to follow progress and evaluate the choice's effect. This considers changes and restorative activities if necessary.

The dynamic cycle can be iterative, especially in powerful business conditions. While checking uncovers that the choice isn't delivering the ideal results, it could be important to return to prior advances, rethink options, and adapt.

Kinds of Business Choices:

Business choices can be grouped into a few classifications in view of their tendency, extension, and effect. A few choices are standard and functional, while others are key, molding the drawn out bearing of an association. Here are a few normal kinds of business choices:

Functional Choices: These choices are everyday and center around the standard exercises of the association. They incorporate choices connected with creation booking, stock administration, worker planning, and quality control.

Strategic Choices: Strategic choices overcome any barrier among functional and key choices. They are worried about the medium-term and frequently include the designation of assets or changes because of market changes. Models incorporate showcasing effort arranging, labor force enhancement, and spending plan allotment.

Key Choices: Key choices have expansive results and impact the general bearing and cutthroat place of an association. These choices are ordinarily made by top administration and address questions connected with market passage, broadening, consolidations and acquisitions, and long haul arranging.

Impromptu Choices: Specially appointed choices are made on an unpredictable premise and frequently in light of explicit, unanticipated conditions. Emergency the executives, answering unforeseen changes on the lookout, or settling debates fall into this classification.

Customized and Non-Modified Choices: Customized choices are monotonous and can be computerized or directed by laid out strategies and methods. Non-modified choices are exceptional, complex, and ordinarily require individualized investigation and judgment.

Dynamic Models:

To work with viable independent direction, different dynamic models and structures have been created. These models give structure, help in understanding the dynamic cycle, and guide leaders in arriving at sound decisions. The following are a couple of outstanding dynamic models:

Levelheaded Dynamic Model: This model accepts that leaders are reasonable and objective, looking to augment utility. It includes an orderly examination of choices, thought of all pertinent data, and an emphasis on accomplishing the most ideal result. While ideal in principle, genuine choices are much of the time affected by mental predispositions and impediments.

Limited Levelheadedness Model: This model perceives that chiefs have restricted time, data, and mental assets. Rather than thoroughly dissecting all other options, leaders in this model satisfice, meaning they pick the main elective that meets their base standards. Limited discernment recognizes that ideal data is seldom achievable.

Natural Dynamic Model: In this model, leaders depend on their impulses, experience, and instinct to decide. While frequently considered to be less precise, instinct can be profoundly important, especially when leaders have skill in a particular space. Natural navigation is fast and is in many cases utilized in circumstances where time is restricted.

Conduct Dynamic Model: This model recognizes that navigation can be affected by mental predispositions, feelings, and social variables. It concentrates on how individuals' ways of behaving and decisions veer off from objective models and tries to comprehend the mental parts of direction.

Emergency Dynamic Model: Emergency navigation is a particular model utilized in high-pressure, time-touchy circumstances. It includes quick issue acknowledgment, gathering fundamental data, and pursuing speedy choices with the accessible information. Emergency direction frequently requires areas of strength for an of initiative and the capacity to oversee pressure.

The decision of which dynamic model to utilize relies upon the unique circumstance, the intricacy of the choice, and the assets accessible. Practically speaking, leaders frequently draw from various models, adjusting their way to deal with suit what is going on.

Challenges in Business Direction:

Business independent direction isn't without its difficulties and intricacies. A few elements can block the capacity to settle on powerful choices. Perceiving these provokes is critical for creating procedures to alleviate them. Here are a few normal difficulties in business direction:

Restricted Data: Chiefs frequently work with deficient or blemished data. Erroneous information, missing information, or vulnerabilities about future occasions can thwart the dynamic interaction.

Mental Predispositions: Chiefs are helpless to mental inclinations, which can prompt mistakes in judgment. Inclinations, for example, tendency to look for predictable answers, securing, and pomposity can impact leaders' insights and decisions.

Time Requirements: Time tension can drive choices to be made quickly, diminishing the chance for intensive investigation and thought of options.

Collective vibes: In cooperative dynamic settings, overall vibes can present difficulties. Mindless conformity, where agreement is focused on over basic assessment, and relational contentions can influence the nature of choices.

Close to home Elements: Feelings, like trepidation, overexcitement, or connection to explicit results, can cloud judgment and lead to poor choices.

Hazard and Vulnerability: Numerous business choices imply inborn dangers and vulnerabilities. Leaders should evaluate and deal with these elements to pursue informed decisions.

Intricacy: The intricacy of present day business conditions can go with choice making more complicated. Interconnected frameworks, globalization, and innovative headways add layers of intricacy to choices.

Moral Situations: Choices might raise moral worries, requiring cautious thought of the moral and social ramifications of the picked strategy.

5.3. Strategies for successful pivots

In the unique scene of business, the capacity to turn is many times a characterizing factor in an association's prosperity. A turn addresses an essential course change, empowering an organization to adjust to changing economic situations, client inclinations, or serious tensions. Fruitful turns can revive a business, cultivate development, and position it for manageable development. In this story, we will investigate the procedures for fruitful turns, looking at their significance, applications in different settings, and the illustrations they give.

The Meaning of Turning:

Turning is an essential reaction to change. It is an acknowledgment that the ongoing plan of action or procedure may presently not be feasible in that frame of mind of developing conditions. Turning includes the boldness to recognize the requirement for change, the nimbleness to adjust rapidly, and the assurance to take advantage of new chances.

The meaning of turning is complex. It permits associations to:

Remain Applicable: In quickly developing ventures, remaining important is basic. Turning assists organizations with staying on top of moving business sector elements, arising advancements, and changing client assumptions.

Answer Difficulties: Turning can address difficulties and misfortunes. Whether an organization is confronting monetary challenges, serious tensions, or functional shortcomings, a top notch turn can give a way to recuperation.

Take advantage of Chances: Turning isn't exclusively about safeguard; it's additionally about offense. By perceiving arising open doors, organizations can turn to gain by recent fads, market specialties, and client requests.

Drive Advancement: Turning frequently prompts development. It urges associations to think inventively, explore different avenues regarding new methodologies, and rock the boat. This inventive soul can saturate a whole association.

Accomplish Practical Development: A fruitful turn can situate an organization for long haul development. By lining up with changing business sector real factors, a turn can make way for feasible extension and productivity.

Upgrade Flexibility: Turning improves an association's versatility. It furnishes an organization with the ability to adjust to unexpected disturbances and keep flourishing in a continually impacting world.

The Turn Range:

Turning is certainly not a one-size-fits-all idea; it exists along a range. The nature and extent of a turn can fluctuate fundamentally, going from gradual changes to revolutionary changes. Here are various focuses along the turn range:

Iterative Turns: Iterative turns include continuous changes in accordance with a current procedure. These progressions are frequently gradual, zeroing in on refining processes, advancing item includes, or venturing into related market portions.

Vital Turns: An essential turn addresses a more significant course change. This might include changes in target markets, item contributions, or center advancements. Vital turns are a reaction to huge changes in the business climate.

Responsive Turns: Receptive turns are provoked by outer tensions or emergencies. These turns might include fast transformations to make due in testing conditions, like a downturn, administrative changes, or an unexpected change in buyer conduct.

Exploratory Turns: Exploratory turns involve a purposeful investigation of new open doors or plans of action. Associations might fan out into adjoining markets, try different things with various income streams, or enhance their contributions.

Revolutionary Turns: Extremist turns are extraordinary in nature. They include a total redesign of the association's plan of action, frequently because of existential dangers or game-evolving developments.

The decision of where to turn on this range relies upon the association's particular conditions, its ability for change, and the idea of the difficulties or open doors it faces.

Techniques for Effective Turns:

Fruitful turns require a thoroughly examined technique, compelling execution, and the capacity to adjust to progressing input and learning. Here are systems to direct associations in accomplishing effective turns:

Careful Appraisal:

Start with an extensive evaluation of the ongoing circumstance. Recognize the variables driving the requirement for a turn, whether it's changing economic situations, declining deals, or serious dangers.

Assess the association's assets, shortcomings, valuable open doors, and dangers (SWOT investigation) to illuminate the turn system.

Accumulate input from all levels of the association and outside partners to acquire assorted viewpoints.

Clear Vision and Reason:

Characterize a reasonable vision for the turn that frames what achievement resembles. Lay out a convincing reason that moves and adjusts the association.

Impart the vision and reason to all partners, guaranteeing that everybody comprehends and embraces the turn's targets.

Information Driven Independent direction:

Base choices on information and bits of knowledge. Lead statistical surveying, client reviews, and cutthroat examinations to illuminate the turn procedure.

Use information to lay out quantifiable objectives and key execution pointers (KPIs) that will follow progress and achievement.

Deft Execution:

Carry out the turn in a coordinated way, considering adaptability and transformation as new data arises.

Break the turn into reasonable stages and achievements, empowering steady advancement.

Asset Assignment:

Apportion assets decisively to help the turn. This might include redistributing financial plans, work force, or mechanical resources.

Guarantee that the fundamental abilities and capacities are accessible to successfully execute the turn.

Client Driven Concentration:

Keep the client at the focal point of the turn. Figure out their necessities, inclinations, and trouble spots to as needs be tailor the turn.

Request client input in the interim and use it to refine the contribution.

Successful Correspondence:

Openness is of the utmost importance. Guarantee that all partners, both interior and outer, are educated regarding the turn and grasp its suggestions.

Be straightforward about the reasoning behind the turn and the normal advantages.

Development and Trial and error:

Energize advancement and trial and error during the turn. Take into consideration reasonable plans of action and testing of groundbreaking thoughts.

Make a culture that embraces gaining from disappointments and iterative improvement.

Observing and Variation:

Persistently screen the advancement of the turn. Survey whether it is accomplishing the ideal outcomes and change as needs be.

Be ready to turn once more, whenever required, in light of the criticism and results.

Supportability:

Think about the drawn out supportability of the turn. Guarantee that the progressions made are not fleeting yet add to the association's continuous achievement.

Assess the turn's effect on the association's central goal, values, and social obligation.

Uses of Effective Turns:

Turns can be applied in different settings, from new companies to laid out partnerships and from private venture undertakings to charitable associations. How about we investigate a few situations where effective turns have been instrumental:

New businesses:

New businesses frequently turn as they gain from beginning business sector input. A turn could include moving starting with one objective market then onto the next, changing the item or administration offering, or modifying the income model.

A model is Slack, which started as a gaming organization called Minuscule Bit. At the point when its down Error didn't build up some decent forward movement, the group turned to make the generally utilized group joint effort instrument, Slack.

Online business:

Online business organizations habitually turn to answer changing shopper inclinations. A turn could include growing item classifications, upgrading the internet shopping experience, or embracing a membership model.

Birchbox, initially a membership based magnificence test administration, turned to underline its internet business store, offering a more extensive scope of excellence items.

Innovation:

Innovation organizations frequently turn in light of movements in the tech scene. This might include adjusting to new stages, embracing arising advances, or entering new business sectors.

Nokia, when a main cell phone producer, turned to zero in on systems administration and media communications gear in the wake of losing ground in the cell phone market.

Charities:

Charitable associations might turn to all the more likely location local area needs or work on their manageability. A turn could include refining program contributions, extending raising money procedures, or changing the hierarchical design.

Show For America, at first a little showing corps, turned to turn into thorough instruction association with more extensive drives.

Retail:

Retail organizations have needed to turn in light of online business rivalry and changing purchaser conduct. Turns could include embracing on the web deals, upgrading the in-store insight, or expanding item contributions.

Best Purchase, a conventional hardware retailer, turned by offering omnichannel retail encounters, growing help contributions, and turning into a player in the web based business space.

Medical care:

Medical care associations might turn to adjust to mechanical headways, changes in persistent socioeconomics, or administrative prerequisites. Turns could include telemedicine reception, the presentation of advanced wellbeing stages, or changes in care models.

Teladoc Wellbeing, initially centered around telehealth for provincial regions, turned to turn into a main telemedicine supplier with an expansive scope of administrations.

Examples from Effective Turns:

Fruitful turns offer important examples for people and associations across various areas. Here are a few key focal points:

Strength and Flexibility: Turning exhibits the significance of versatility and flexibility. Associations that can change direction because of changing circumstances are better prepared to climate vulnerabilities.

Embracing Change: Turns highlight the benefit of perceiving the requirement for change and embracing it instead of opposing it. Change is a consistent in business, and the people who can adjust rapidly flourish.

5.4. Learning from failure

Disappointment is a widespread encounter, rising above limits and influencing individuals in varying social statuses. It is an unavoidable piece of the human condition, influencing people, associations, and social orders. Regardless of the unfortunate underlying meanings frequently connected with disappointment, it very well may be a strong impetus for learning and development. In this account, we will investigate the idea of gaining from disappointment, analyzing its importance, its applications in different spaces, and the significant examples it confers.

The Meaning of Gaining from Disappointment:

Disappointment is frequently viewed as something to be stayed away from, a wellspring of disgrace or frustration. Notwithstanding, a developing collection of examination and incalculable examples of overcoming adversity confirm the meaning of gaining from disappointment. Here are a few justifications for why embracing disappointment as a learning opportunity is fundamental:

Versatility Building: Disappointment can be a cauldron for flexibility. It tests a person's or an association's capacity to quickly return, adjust, and continue on even with difficulty.

Advancement and Imagination: Numerous forward leaps and developments have been conceived out of disappointment. At the point when people or groups face difficulties, they frequently need to think imaginatively to track down new arrangements.

Expertise Improvement: Disappointment can uncover holes in abilities or information. It gives a stage to distinguishing regions needing improvement and the inspiration to foster new capabilities.

Risk-Showing and Drive: Embracing disappointment empowers risk-showing and drive. At the point when the apprehension about disappointment is decreased, individuals and associations are more ready to investigate an unknown area and seek after aggressive objectives.

Self-Reflection and Variation: Disappointment requires self-reflection. People and associations can break down what turned out badly, gain from their slip-ups, and adjust their systems likewise.

Modesty and Sympathy: Disappointment cultivates lowliness and compassion. It advises us that everybody faces difficulties, and it can prompt a more noteworthy comprehension of the battles and mishaps of others.

Long haul Achievement: Gaining from disappointment is in many cases a venturing stone to long haul achievement. People and associations that can turn and adjust are better situated to flourish in a quickly impacting world.

Self-awareness: On an individual level, disappointment can be an impetus for significant development. It can prompt expanded mindfulness, the improvement of strength, and the quest for additional significant objectives.

The Range of Disappointment:

Disappointment exists along a range, going from minor difficulties to significant emergencies. Understanding where a specific disappointment falls on this range is significant for evaluating its suggestions and the potential for learning. Here are various focuses along the range of disappointment:

Minor Disappointments: These are regular mishaps, blunders, or slip-ups that have insignificant outcomes. They give chances to learning without really hurting.

Moderate Disappointments: Moderate disappointments have a more articulated influence and may bring about monetary misfortunes, botched open doors, or harmed connections. These disappointments can be important for development when seen as opportunities for growth.

Significant Disappointments: Significant disappointments are huge misfortunes that can have expansive results. They might prompt monetary emergencies, business terminations, or profession difficulties. Gaining from significant disappointments can be especially difficult yet in addition colossally important.

Disastrous Disappointments: Horrendous disappointments are outrageous and can prompt decimating results. These disappointments might include wellbeing emergencies, cataclysmic events, or fundamental breakdowns. Gaining from disastrous disappointments frequently requires a significant reconsideration of one's life or hierarchical qualities.

The potential for gaining from disappointment exists across this range, however the cycle and the profundity of learning can differ fundamentally.

Procedures for Gaining from Disappointment:

Gaining from disappointment is certainly not a programmed interaction; it requires goal and reflection. Here are procedures to work with powerful gaining from disappointment:

Recognize Disappointment: The initial step is recognizing and tolerating disappointment. Keep away from refusal, fault, or evasion, as these responses can impede the educational experience.

Self-Reflection: Take part in self-reflection to grasp the purposes for the disappointment. Ask yourself what added to the result, what might have been done another way, and what examples can be gathered.

Look for Input: Support transparent criticism from others, like tutors, companions, or partners. They can give significant experiences and viewpoints.

Embrace a Development Mentality: Take on a development outlook, which accepts that capacities and knowledge can be created through exertion and learning. This attitude energizes flexibility notwithstanding misfortunes.

Set Practical Assumptions: Disappointment is a piece of the cycle, and mishaps are inescapable. Setting practical assumptions can help people and associations better adapt to and gain from disappointments.

Emphasize and Examination: When faced with disappointment, view it as a chance to repeat and investigation. Attempt new methodologies and test various systems to address the difficulties.

Center around Arrangements: Focus on tracking down arrangements and options, instead of harping on the actual issue. Utilize the illustrations from inability to illuminate future activities.

Remain Committed: Determination is vital to gaining from disappointment. It's vital for stay focused on private or authoritative objectives and keep making progress toward them.

Share Examples: Offer the illustrations gained from disappointment with others. By sharing, you help other people as well as build up your own learning.

Uses of Gaining from Disappointment:

The idea of gaining from disappointment is relevant in different settings, from self-awareness to hierarchical achievement. Here are a few situations where gaining from disappointment is especially pertinent:

New companies and Business venture:

In the realm of new businesses and business venture, disappointment is normal. Business people frequently face monetary misfortunes, market dismissal, and item disappointments. Gaining from these encounters is basic for future achievement.

Advancement and Exploration:

In examination and advancement, disappointment is innate during the time spent revelation. Numerous notable logical advances and creations arose out of trial and error and iterative disappointment.

Project The executives:
Project administrators regularly experience difficulties and surprising impediments. Gaining from the disappointment of an undertaking or explicit errands can prompt superior venture the board rehearses.

Schooling and Self-awareness:
Gaining from disappointment is fundamental to instruction and self-improvement. Understudies frequently face scholastic mishaps, and people experience individual and expert difficulties that give amazing chances to learning.

Initiative and The board:
Pioneers and supervisors should explore complex circumstances and pursue hard decisions. Gaining from disappointments in authority can improve direction and group the board abilities.

Authoritative Culture:
An association's way of life assumes a critical part in how disappointment is seen. Developing a culture that embraces gaining from disappointment can encourage advancement and versatility.

Medical care and Medication:
In medical care, clinical experts gain from instances of therapy that didn't accomplish the ideal results. This learning adds to enhancements in clinical practices and patient consideration.

Illustrations from Gaining from Disappointment:
Gaining from disappointment bestows important examples that stretch out past private and expert turn of events. Here are key action items:

Versatility: Gaining from disappointment assembles strength, the capacity to quickly return and adjust to misfortune. Strength is a priceless fundamental ability.

Advancement and Inventiveness: Disappointment supports development and innovative critical thinking. It prompts people and associations to think diversely and foster new arrangements.

Humble Certainty: Gaining from disappointment develops a feeling of humble certainty. It recognizes that misfortunes are a piece of development yet imparts trust in the capacity to beat difficulties.

Sympathy: Disappointment encourages compassion by lowering people and helping them to remember the battles of others. This sympathy can further develop connections and cooperation.

Nonstop Improvement: Gaining from disappointment is a course of persistent improvement. It urges people and associations to look for better approaches to getting things done and to repeat their methodologies.

Risk-Taking: Embracing disappointment energizes determined risk-taking. It empowers people and associations to investigate open doors that might have been viewed as excessively hazardous before.

Flexibility: Gaining from disappointment improves versatility. It prepares people and associations to explore change and vulnerability.

Objective Lucidity: Disappointment frequently explains objectives and needs. It powers people and associations to reexamine their goals and settle on additional deliberate decisions.

Chapter 6

Scaling and Growth

Scaling and development are basic ideas in the realm of business, innovation, and, surprisingly, in the domain of human turn of events. These terms address the extension and movement of frameworks, associations, and people. They are unyieldingly connected, as development frequently requires endlessly scaling, thusly, powers development. In this story, we will investigate the complicated connection among scaling and development across different spaces, stressing the hidden standards, difficulties, and valuable open doors that emerge.

One can't dive into the subject of scaling and development without first tending to the setting of business. In the corporate scene, scaling alludes to the most common way of expanding the size, reach, or extent of an endeavor. This can include extending tasks, expanding the client base, or differentiating item and administration contributions. Development, then again, is the result of effective scaling, bringing about the extension of income, piece of the pie, and benefit. Scaling is an essential decision, and when executed really, it catalyzes development.

One of the most unmistakable instances of scaling and development in business is Amazon. The internet business monster, established by Jeff Bezos in 1994 as a web-based book shop, has turned into a worldwide behemoth with different business fragments, including distributed computing, diversion, and man-made consciousness. Amazon's steady spotlight on scaling, from its broad satisfaction organization to its Superb enrollment program, has driven dramatic development, making it perhaps of the most significant organization on the planet.

In innovation, the connection among scaling and development is significantly more articulated. Moore's Regulation, instituted by Gordon Moore, prime supporter of Intel, sets that the quantity of semiconductors on a CPU would twofold roughly like clockwork. This expectation has turned out as expected for a really long time and has been the main impetus behind the dramatic development of processing power. Downsizing the size of semiconductors while expanding their number has empowered the innovation business to grow quicker, more modest, and all the more impressive gadgets, prompting amazing development in applications, like computerized reasoning, versatile processing, and the Web of Things.

Nonetheless, this determined quest for scaling in the innovation area has not come without difficulties. The fast advancement of equipment and programming has raised worries about information security, protection, and the computerized partition. As innovation scales, so do the dangers and moral contemplations. Finding some kind of harmony between scaling for development and guaranteeing capable development stays a squeezing worry for the business.

Past the corporate and mechanical domains, scaling and development assume a vital part in the improvement of countries and social orders. Monetary development is a vital measurement for estimating a country's advancement. State run administrations carry out strategies and drives pointed toward scaling different areas, from framework to instruction, with a definitive objective of accomplishing supportable financial development. The connection among scaling and development is obvious in the progress of many non-industrial nations into developing business sectors and, at last, created countries.

China's change throughout the course of recent many years is a demonstration of this association. Through essential scaling endeavors, including framework advancement, unfamiliar ventures, and exchange development, China has seen remarkable monetary development. Its combination into the worldwide economy and the scaling of its assembling and innovation areas have impelled it to turn into the world's second-biggest economy. This striking scaling-to-development venture has lifted countless individuals out of neediness and reshaped the worldwide financial scene.

In the domain of self-improvement, scaling and development are characteristically connected. As people, we continually try to scale our capacities, information, and encounters to accomplish individual and expert development. This excursion isn't not normal for that of organizations or countries. Scaling for self-awareness could include acquiring new abilities, taking on additional obligations, or expanding one's viewpoints through movement and investigation. As people scale, they unavoidably experience self-improvement, turning out to be more competent and versatile.

The tale of Elon Musk fills in as a convincing delineation of individual scaling and development. Musk, the visionary business person behind SpaceX and Tesla, ceaselessly pushes the limits of what is conceivable. He scales his desires by wandering into a strange area, for example, business space travel and manageable energy. Musk's resolute obligation to scaling his endeavors has brought about both mechanical headways and huge monetary development. His work encapsulates the idea of self-improvement driven by tireless scaling.

Scaling and development are additionally integral to the regular world. Natural frameworks, from cells to environments, show examples of scaling. The scaling regulations in science uncover that as creatures expansion in size, different characteristics, for example, metabolic rate and pulse, follow unsurprising scaling connections. For instance, bigger creatures will generally have more slow metabolic rates per unit of weight, while more modest creatures have quicker rates. These scaling connections support the development and working of organic frameworks.

The idea of scaling in science reaches out past people to whole environments. Environmental scaling looks at the connections between the size and variety of biological systems and their efficiency and soundness. Scaling regulations in biology assist us with understanding how the development and improvement of biological systems are affected by factors like species variety, energy stream, and supplement cycling. By concentrating on these scaling connections, environmentalists can settle on additional educated conclusions about preservation, asset the board, and the manageability of our planet.

Scaling and development are not without their difficulties and constraints. In the business world, scaling excessively fast or without a strong groundwork can prompt overextension, monetary shakiness, and at last, disappointment. New companies that experience quick scaling without a relating expansion in income frequently end up in shaky circumstances. Accomplishing feasible development frequently requires a sensitive harmony between scaling desires and monetary reasonability.

The innovation area faces comparable difficulties. The speed of mechanical change is fast to the point that keeping up, prompting worries about outdated nature and innovative debt can be troublesome. Scaling framework and administrations without sufficient thought for security and moral ramifications can bring about weaknesses and potentially negative results.

On a worldwide scale, the quest for monetary development can prompt ecological corruption, asset exhaustion, and social disparities. Finding some kind of harmony between scaling monetary exercises and keeping up with maintainability is a perplexing test looked by states and associations around the world.

Individual scaling for development additionally presents obstacles. People might encounter burnout, stress, and an absence of balance between fun and serious activities while propelling themselves too hard as they continued looking for individual and expert development. Finding the right speed and equilibrium is urgent for supported self-awareness.

Indeed, even in the regular world, scaling has its cutoff points. Organic entities, biological systems, and conditions can scale such a long ways prior to experiencing requirements. These limitations might be forced by the accessibility of assets, natural circumstances, or the laws of material science. Understanding these impediments is basic for safeguarding the sensitive harmony between environments and monitoring biodiversity.

As of late, there has been developing acknowledgment of the requirement for manageable scaling and development in all areas. Maintainability, in this unique situation, alludes to the capacity to scale and develop while limiting adverse consequences on the climate, society, and people in the future. Organizations are progressively taking on manageable practices, for example, sustainable power sources and roundabout economy standards, to offset their development aspirations with ecological obligation.

The innovation area is likewise gaining ground in maintainability. Green innovation drives expect to decrease the natural impression of the business by advancing energy-proficient equipment, clean energy sources, and dependable removal of electronic waste. The progress to economical scaling and development is driven by a developing familiarity with the need to address environmental change and diminish the ecological effect of innovation.

On a worldwide scale, manageability is a center thought chasing financial development. Numerous countries are embracing maintainable improvement objectives and approaches to guarantee that their development directions are naturally dependable and socially comprehensive. Offsetting monetary development with social value and ecological conservation is an imposing test, however one that is fundamental for the prosperity of present and people in the future.

6.1. Achieving profitability

Accomplishing productivity is a key objective for organizations across different enterprises and areas. Productivity is the bedrock whereupon the supportability and progress of an organization are fabricated. It mirrors the capacity to produce more income than costs, at last prompting monetary security, development, and the capacity to reinvest in the business. In this story, we will dig profound into the complex parts of accomplishing productivity in the cutting edge business scene, investigating methodologies, challenges, and the powerful idea of this significant undertaking.

Benefit depends on the capacity of a business to really deal with its monetary assets, create income, and control costs. To accomplish productivity, organizations frequently utilize a multi-layered approach that incorporates various features of their tasks. One of the essential methodologies for accomplishing benefit includes income age, which can take different structures, including expanding deals, extending the client base, and enhancing item or administration contributions.

Deals development is a critical driver of productivity. This can be achieved through showcasing and deals endeavors that increment brand perceivability, draw in new clients, and hold existing ones. Furthermore, deals development can be accomplished by venturing into new business sectors or locales, either locally or universally. By taking advantage of new client fragments, organizations can reinforce their income streams, which is fundamental for productivity.

Extending the client base is one more urgent part of income age. This can be accomplished through successful promoting and client obtaining procedures. Client securing envelops many exercises, from publicizing and advancements to client relationship the board. A faithful client base can fundamentally add to long haul benefit through recurrent business and informal exchange references.

Differentiating item or administration contributions is one more method for improving income and productivity. Organizations frequently acquaint new items or administrations with catch a more extensive piece of the pie and take care of changing shopper inclinations. Expansion can decrease the dependence on a solitary item or administration, making the business stronger to showcase variances and monetary slumps.

Cost control is similarly critical chasing productivity. Organizations should deal with their costs wisely to guarantee that expenses don't surpass income. This includes investigating each aspect of tasks, from creation and coordinated factors to above and managerial costs. Cost-cutting measures might incorporate advancing inventory network the board, lessening waste, and embracing innovation answers for further develop effectiveness.

Proficiency acquires through innovation are especially huge in the cutting edge business scene. Robotization, information examination, and distributed computing have upset the manner in which organizations work. Robotization, for example, can smooth out routine undertakings, further develop precision, and decrease work costs. Information examination offer significant bits of knowledge into client conduct and market patterns, helping organizations in going with informed choices. Distributed computing gives practical and adaptable framework, disposing of the requirement for broad capital interests in IT.

In the journey for benefit, organizations should likewise think about valuing methodologies. Setting the right cost for items or administrations is a fragile equilibrium. Overpricing can drive away clients, while undervaluing may prompt diminished net revenues. Organizations utilize different evaluating techniques, for example, cost-in addition to estimating, esteem based valuing, and dynamic valuing, to adjust their estimating to client assumptions and economic situations.

Moreover, accomplishing benefit includes a sharp comprehension of the serious scene. Statistical surveying is crucial for handle the elements of one's industry and recognize open doors and dangers. Organizations need to separate themselves by offering remarkable incentives, unrivaled quality, or uncommon client care to remain in front of the opposition. A very much created cutthroat technique could drive income at any point as well as improve costs, prompting higher benefit.

Business venture and advancement are characteristic for accomplishing productivity. Business visionaries frequently try to upset customary business sectors by presenting imaginative items or administrations. By recognizing neglected requirements or shortcomings, business visionaries can cut out specialties that take into account higher net revenues. The course of development may likewise include working on existing items or administrations to acquire an upper hand.

An eminent illustration of business and development in accomplishing productivity is the ascent of ride-sharing organizations like Uber and Lyft. These organizations utilized innovation to make another market portion by giving helpful, on-request transportation administrations. Their troublesome plans of action tested customary taxi benefits and upset metropolitan transportation, prompting critical productivity.

The job of consumer loyalty in productivity couldn't possibly be more significant. Fulfilled clients are bound to become recurrent purchasers and backers for a brand. Building major areas of strength for a driven culture is fundamental for accomplishing productivity. Organizations need to put resources into client care, pay attention to client input, and constantly further develop the client experience to cultivate devotion and drive long haul benefit.

Globalization has opened up new roads for accomplishing productivity. The capacity to arrive at global business sectors has extended the development potential for organizations, everything being equal. Worldwide partnerships have utilized worldwide stockpile chains to streamline costs, while internet business has made it workable for even independent ventures to take advantage of global business sectors. The intricacy of global business, notwithstanding, brings its own arrangement of difficulties, including administrative consistence, money changes, and social subtleties.

Productivity can likewise be affected by the more extensive financial climate. Monetary circumstances, like downturns or times of expansion, can affect buyer spending, creation expenses, and financing costs. Organizations should be versatile and nimble to actually explore these changes. Risk the board methodologies, for example, expanding income sources and keeping a sound money hold, can assist with moderating the effect of financial changes on productivity.

In the present progressively computerized world, online presence and web based business have become instrumental in accomplishing benefit. The ascent of online business stages has changed the retail scene, empowering organizations to arrive at a worldwide client base with lower above costs contrasted with physical stores. Laying out a vigorous internet based presence, remembering an internet business site and a presence for web-based entertainment, is fundamental for organizations hoping to improve their benefit.

The help business, as well, has seen a significant shift toward online administrations and computerized stages. The appearance of the sharing economy, encapsulated by organizations like Airbnb and TaskRabbit, has upset conventional assistance models. These stages empower people to offer administrations or lease their resources, like homes or vehicles, making new revenue sources and valuable open doors for benefit.

In the monetary area, accomplishing benefit is intently attached to speculation methodologies and portfolio the executives. Monetary establishments, including banks, venture companies, and insurance agency, produce income through premium on advances, speculation returns, and expenses. Compelling portfolio the executives and chance appraisal are basic in enhancing benefit while overseeing openness to possible monetary slumps.

Land likewise assumes a critical part in benefit. Property possession and speculation can turn out rental revenue and appreciation in property estimation. Land engineers and financial backers utilize methodologies to improve the benefit of their portfolios, whether through property advancement, property the executives, or long haul speculations.

Maintainability and corporate social obligation have arisen as basic parts of accomplishing productivity in the 21st hundred years. Customers and financial backers are progressively aware of the natural and social effect of organizations. Organizations that embrace economical practices, diminish their carbon impression, and take part in moral business direct frequently appreciate reputational benefits, client dedication, and admittance to ecologically cognizant business sectors.

An imperative outline of manageability's effect on benefit is the change to sustainable power sources. Organizations that put resources into sustainable power advancements diminish their ecological effect as well as frequently benefit from lower energy costs in the long haul. Additionally, customers are progressively picking items and administrations from organizations focused on supportability, encouraging brand devotion and driving benefit.

Accomplishing benefit, be that as it may, isn't without its difficulties and expected entanglements. Chasing income development, organizations might depend on forceful evaluating procedures that undermine their overall revenues. These techniques might draw in clients at first, however the powerlessness to take care of expenses and produce benefits can prompt monetary unsteadiness and, at last, business disappointment.

Overseeing costs is another unpredictable errand. Reducing expenses aimlessly can prompt quality issues, decreased worker spirit, and, surprisingly, legitimate issues. It's vital for figure out some kind of harmony between cost-cutting and keeping up with the nature of items and administrations.

Market instability and contest can likewise present critical difficulties to productivity. Quick changes in buyer inclinations, mechanical headways, or the development of problematic contenders can disturb laid out organizations. Keeping up with benefit under such circumstances requires dexterity.

6.2. Scaling the business operations

Scaling business tasks is a basic part of development and outcome in the corporate world. Whether you're a startup expecting to grow quickly or a laid out organization trying to increment piece of the pie, scaling is a mind boggling and multi-layered try. It includes a key and methodical way to deal with guarantee that the different features of a business can develop flawlessly to oblige expanded request, while keeping up with effectiveness, quality, and benefit. In this thorough investigation, we will dive into the complexities of scaling business tasks, taking into account the methodologies, difficulties, and dynamic nature of this significant cycle.

The Underpinnings of Scaling

To set out on the excursion of scaling business tasks, it is vital for first establish areas of strength for a. This establishment incorporates having a reasonable comprehension of your plan of action, market, and clients. Before you scale, you should lay out a strong item market fit. All in all, your item or administration ought to be generally welcomed and take care of the necessities and inclinations of your main interest group.

In addition, the versatility of your plan of action ought to be a critical thought all along. Versatility alludes to your capacity to deal with an expansion popular without a relative expansion in assets or expenses. A plan of action that can undoubtedly oblige development, both in an upward direction and evenly, is better situated for effective scaling.

For instance, programming as-a-administration (SaaS) organizations frequently have profoundly versatile plans of action. Their items are facilitated in the cloud, making it simple to oblige extra clients with negligible framework venture. This adaptability permits SaaS organizations to scale proficiently as they develop their client base.

Methodologies for Scaling Business Tasks

Functional Proficiency: Prior to scaling, you should streamline your current tasks. This includes smoothing out processes, lessening waste, and upgrading efficiency. Executing lean procedures and robotization can assist you with accomplishing more with less.

Market Development: One of the most well-known techniques for scaling is venturing into new business sectors. This could include entering new geographic locales, focusing on new client fragments, or expanding product offerings to take care of a more extensive crowd. Effective market extension requires exhaustive statistical surveying, social awareness, and a comprehension of neighborhood guidelines.

Diversifying and Permitting: For specific organizations, diversifying or authorizing can be a versatile model. By permitting different business people to duplicate your business under your image, you can grow quickly without the requirement for huge capital venture.

Vital Organizations: Teaming up with different organizations can be a strong method for scaling. Whether it's through joint endeavors, vital coalitions, or associations, you can use each other's assets and assets to become together.

Online Presence and Web based business: In the computerized age, having major areas of strength for a presence is fundamental for scaling. Web based business stages empower organizations to contact a worldwide crowd and oblige expanded request effortlessly. Viable computerized advertising techniques can drive development in the web-based space.

Acquisitions and Consolidations: Development through obtaining or consolidation is a deep rooted system. By procuring or converging with different organizations, you can quickly acquire piece of the pie, obtain new innovations or items, and grow your tasks.

Speculation and Financing: Scaling frequently requires capital venture. This can emerge out of different sources, including funding, confidential value, bank credits, or beginning public contributions (Initial public offerings). Getting the right subsidizing is fundamental for executing your scaling procedure.

Every one of these scaling methodologies has its benefits and difficulties. The decision of technique ought to line up with your plan of action, objectives, and the common economic situations. Moreover, scaling is seldom a direct cycle. It can include a blend of these techniques as your business develops.

The Difficulties of Scaling

Scaling business tasks isn't without its difficulties, and perceiving and tending to these difficulties is imperative for fruitful scaling. A portion of the normal difficulties include:

Keeping up with Quality: As tasks grow, keeping up with a similar degree of value can be a test. Consistency is fundamental to maintain your image's standing. This frequently requires distinct cycles, preparing, and quality control measures.

Asset Designation: Overseeing assets productively is critical. Scaling frequently requires huge interests in framework, innovation, and HR. Designating these assets successfully to help development without causing strain is a fragile difficult exercise.

Social and Authoritative Changes: Scaling can achieve social and hierarchical movements. It's critical to guarantee that the way of life of your organization stays in one piece or develops in a positive manner. Furthermore, changes in hierarchical construction and the board practices might be important to help development.

Store network and Strategies: Growing activities can strain your store network and coordinated operations. Overseeing expanded request, obtaining materials, and conveying items or administrations on time become more perplexing. Improving store network activities is critical to scaling.

Administrative Consistence: Working in numerous business sectors or districts frequently includes consistence with assorted guidelines. Exploring legitimate and administrative obstacles is a test that requires skill and flexibility.

Innovation and Foundation: As request increments, innovation framework necessities to keep up. This incorporates the equipment as well as programming frameworks, network safety measures, and information the executives. Versatile innovation arrangements are crucial for help development.

Ability Securing and Maintenance: Drawing in and holding top ability turns out to be more basic as your business scales. Rivalry for gifted representatives can be wild, and offering serious pay, benefits, and a positive workplace is fundamental.

Income The executives: Fast development can strain your income. Expanded costs to help scaling might dominate the income produced temporarily. Viable income the executives is significant to guarantee monetary strength during the scaling system.

Consumer loyalty: A bigger client base carries with it more different requirements and assumptions. Guaranteeing that clients keep on being happy with your items or administrations is a consistent test. Great client care and input systems are essential.

Contest and Interruption: The business scene is dynamic, and contenders or disruptors may arise out of the blue. Remaining deft and constantly enhancing is critical to hold an upper hand.

Contextual analyses in Scaling

A few organizations act as unmistakable contextual investigations in effective scaling. Amazon, for example, started as an internet based book shop and scaled its tasks to turn into the world's biggest online business stage, offering a large number of items and administrations, including distributed computing through Amazon Web Administrations (AWS).

Uber is one more imperative instance of scaling. The ride-sharing organization changed metropolitan transportation by utilizing innovation to interface drivers and riders. Uber extended its administrations to various nations, ceaselessly advancing and adjusting to nearby guidelines and social contrasts.

Airbnb is a superb outline of how scaling can upset conventional enterprises. The organization began by leasing pneumatic beds in an extra room and scaled its foundation to offer facilities in excess of 220 nations. Airbnb's plan of action difficulties the customary lodging industry by empowering people to lease their homes and properties to voyagers.

These contextual analyses feature the different techniques and difficulties related with scaling business activities. Amazon zeroed in on broadening its item contributions and utilizing innovation, Uber ventured into new geographic business sectors, and Airbnb upset the housing business by associating hosts and explorers through a web-based stage.

The Job of Innovation in Scaling

Innovation assumes a focal part in scaling business tasks in the cutting edge period. It is an empowering influence, an impetus, and a driver of development. The following are a few critical manners by which innovation adds to scaling:

Robotization: Computerization of normal and monotonous undertakings diminishes the requirement for broad human work as a business scales. This upgrades proficiency as well as diminishes functional expenses.

Information Examination: Information investigation gives significant experiences into client conduct, market patterns, and functional execution. It empowers information driven independent direction, which is essential for powerful scaling.

Distributed computing: Distributed computing offers adaptable and savvy foundation. Organizations can undoubtedly extend their IT assets depending on the situation, without the requirement for broad capital speculation.

Online business Stages: Online business stages furnish organizations with a worldwide reach, empowering them to serve clients all over the planet. Online commercial centers and computerized retail facades work on the most common way of coming to and offering to a more extensive crowd.

Versatile Innovations: Portable advancements and applications empower organizations to associate with clients and representatives in a more customized and productive way. Scaling tasks frequently includes streamlining for portable access.

Large Information and AI: Enormous information and AI innovations take into consideration the examination of huge datasets and the robotization of mind boggling errands. These advancements can further develop client encounters, streamline supply chains, and improve direction.

Online protection: As organizations scale, they become more vulnerable to network safety dangers. Innovation is fundamental for executing powerful network safety measures to safeguard information, framework, and client data.

6.3. Gaining market share

Acquiring piece of the pie is a principal objective for organizations across different ventures. It mirrors the level of the complete market that an organization or item catches and is a significant mark of a business' serious position and development potential. In this top to bottom investigation, we will dig into the complexities of acquiring piece of the pie, looking at the techniques, challenges, and the powerful idea of this fundamental pursuit.

Understanding Portion of the overall industry

Piece of the pie is a metric that evaluates an organization's or alternately item's deals as a level of the complete market's deals inside a particular industry or area. It is a fundamental benchmark for evaluating a business' presentation and seriousness. Piece of the pie can be determined in view of income, units sold, or other pertinent measurements, and it gives bits of knowledge into an organization's overall standing contrasted with its rivals.

An organization with a high piece of the pie is viewed as a market chief, frequently getting a charge out of benefits like economies of scale, memorability, and client dependability. Then again, organizations with lower pieces of the pie should utilize different systems to make strides, challenge occupants, and develop their cut of the market.

Methodologies for Acquiring Piece of the pie

Item Separation: One of the critical methodologies for acquiring portion of the overall industry is item separation. By offering special elements, better quality, or creative arrangements, a business can separate itself from contenders. Clients are bound to pick an item that hangs out on the lookout.

Value Seriousness: Contending on cost is a typical methodology, particularly in cost touchy business sectors. By offering items or administrations at a lower cost while keeping up with quality, an organization can draw in cost cognizant clients.

Market Extension: Venturing into new geographic areas or focusing on various client portions can be a successful method for acquiring piece of the pie. Enhancing your market presence can open new income streams.

Acquisitions and Consolidations: Obtaining or converging with different organizations is an essential move to acquire portion of the overall industry rapidly. It permits a business to combine assets and client bases, eventually expanding its presence on the lookout.

Key Associations: Working together with different organizations can improve your portion of the overall industry. By shaping associations or coalitions, organizations can use each other's assets and client bases to infiltrate new business sectors or upgrade their seriousness.

Advancement and Exploration and Improvement: Putting resources into innovative work (Research and development) and advancement can bring about new, cutthroat items or administrations. This draws in new clients as well as holds existing ones, prompting expanded piece of the pie.

Showcasing and Advancement: Compelling advertising and advancement procedures can assist with making brand mindfulness and draw in clients. Using promoting, advertising, and advanced showcasing can fundamentally influence piece of the pie.

Client Driven Approach: Zeroing in on consumer loyalty and giving great client care can prompt recurrent business and client dependability. Fulfilled clients are bound to stay faithful and prescribe your image to other people, adding to piece of the pie development.

Quality Confirmation and Ceaseless Improvement: Reliably conveying top notch items or administrations assembles trust and validity on the lookout. Organizations that keep a promise to quality frequently experience consistent development in piece of the pie.

Maintainable Practices: Supportable and ecologically dependable strategic approaches are mean a lot to customers. Organizations that embrace manageable practices draw in ecologically cognizant clients as well as advantage from positive brand picture, which can prompt expanded piece of the pie.

Challenges in Acquiring Piece of the pie

Acquiring portion of the overall industry isn't without its difficulties, and organizations should explore different hindrances to make progress:

Extraordinary Contest: Seeking portion of the overall industry frequently implies going toward deep rooted and forceful contenders. Defeating these opponents can be a huge test.

Market Immersion: In mature business sectors, where numerous organizations as of now have a significant piece of the pie, finding space for development can be troublesome. Presenting new items or administrations that stand apart becomes fundamental.

Client Devotion: Client reliability to existing brands can be a considerable obstacle. Persuading clients to change from a believed brand to a novice requires a convincing offer.

Administrative and Consistence Difficulties: Various business sectors might have fluctuating guidelines and consistence necessities that can present hindrances to extension. Complying with these principles and guidelines is essential yet can be intricate and exorbitant.

Monetary Variances: Financial slumps can influence customer spending and buying choices. During downturns or monetary emergencies, acquiring piece of the pie can especially challenge.

Inventory network and Coordinated operations: Guaranteeing the accessibility of items or administrations, particularly while scaling, can be a strategies challenge. Productive store network the executives is urgent for fulfilling market needs.

Mechanical Progressions: Fast innovative headways can upset markets and plans of action. Organizations should ceaselessly advance and adjust to stay cutthroat.

Value Wars: Contending on cost can prompt cost wars, which might disintegrate overall revenues. Keeping a harmony between serious estimating and productivity is a sensitive errand.

Contextual analyses in Acquiring Piece of the pie

A few organizations have utilized effective procedures to acquire portion of the overall industry. The accompanying contextual analyses show how various organizations have moved toward this test:

Netflix: Netflix, a membership based web-based feature, is a perfect representation of an organization that acquired critical portion of the overall industry through development. By presenting an immense library of on-request satisfied at cutthroat costs, it disturbed the customary digital media business. Netflix put vigorously in creating unique substance, which further pulled in endorsers and permitted it to catch a huge portion of the worldwide streaming business sector.

Tesla: Tesla, an electric vehicle producer, entered the car market and acquired piece of the pie by zeroing in on advancement and item separation. Its obligation to delivering top notch electric vehicles with state of the art innovation, excellent execution, and reasonable highlights put it aside from conventional automakers. Tesla's quick extension was driven by client interest for electric vehicles and its obligation to ecological maintainability.

Amazon: Amazon, at first a web-based book shop, differentiated its item reach and client base to turn into a worldwide internet business goliath. Its technique included serious valuing, proficient coordinated operations, and a client driven approach. Through essential acquisitions and organizations, Amazon ventured into new business sectors, for example, distributed computing (Amazon Web Administrations) and shrewd home gadgets (Amazon Reverberation), further expanding its piece of the pie.

The Job of Computerized Change in Acquiring Piece of the pie

Computerized change has turned into a critical impetus for acquiring piece of the pie in the present business scene. It includes the coordination of computerized advancements into different parts of a business to drive development, further develop tasks, upgrade client encounters, and increment seriousness. Advanced change techniques include:

Web based business Stages: The development of web based shopping and web based business stages has been a groundbreaking power in numerous ventures. Organizations that take on and streamline internet business channels can arrive at a more extensive client base and gain piece of the pie.

Information Examination and man-made intelligence: Bridling the force of information investigation and computerized reasoning (simulated intelligence) permits organizations to go with information driven choices, grasp client conduct, and anticipate market patterns. This knowledge helps in fitting items, administrations, and promoting methodologies to catch piece of the pie.

Portable Applications and Openness: Creating versatile applications that empower clients to cooperate with a business on their cell phones has become fundamental. Versatile applications further develop client commitment, accommodation, and availability, adding to portion of the overall industry development.

Distributed computing: Cloud-based arrangements give adaptability, deftness, and cost-adequacy. They empower organizations to extend quickly and productively, assisting with catching portion of the overall industry.

Advanced Promoting and Virtual Entertainment: Successful computerized showcasing efforts, online entertainment procedures, and content advertising endeavors can construct brand mindfulness, draw in clients, and add to piece of the pie development.

Robotization and Advanced mechanics: Carrying out computerization and advanced mechanics in assembling, coordinated factors, and client support cycles can prompt expanded productivity, decreased costs, and the capacity to fulfill developing need.

Blockchain Innovation: In ventures, for example, money and store network, blockchain innovation is being utilized to improve straightforwardness, security, and trust, which can prompt acquiring piece of the pie by drawing in organizations and clients searching for secure and dependable arrangements.

The Significance of Client Centricity in Acquiring Piece of the pie

A client driven approach is urgent to acquiring and holding portion of the overall industry. Client centricity places clients at the focal point of a business' system and tasks. Here are key parts of a client driven approach:

Understanding Client Needs: Organizations should completely grasp their clients, their inclinations, and their trouble spots. Directing statistical surveying, overviews, and criticism examination helps in acquiring experiences into client needs.

Personalization: Altering items, administrations, and advertising messages in view of individual client inclinations can upgrade the client experience. Personalization causes clients to feel esteemed and comprehended.

6.4. Disrupting industries and creating impact

Disturbing ventures and making a critical effect is a significant and groundbreaking interaction. It includes shaking things up, reconsidering conventional plans of action, and spearheading inventive ways to deal with tackle existing issues. In this exhaustive investigation, we will dig into the elements of disturbing ventures, analyzing the methodologies, challenges, and the extensive ramifications of reshaping markets and making enduring change.

Grasping Industry Interruption

Industry interruption alludes to the major change of laid out business sectors and plans of action through development and novel methodologies. It frequently includes the presentation of new innovations, items, or administrations that challenge existing standards and rethink industry principles. Disturbance can rise out of the two new businesses and laid out organizations ready to split away from the regular approach to carrying on with work.

Disruptors normally intend to offer better benefit than clients by tending to neglected needs, diminishing expenses, or improving accommodation. This quest for advancement can prompt the relocation of occupant players, as clients shift their faithfulness and spending towards troublesome arrangements. Industry disturbance can make huge monetary and cultural effect.

Systems for Upsetting Ventures

Upsetting enterprises requires a blend of inventive systems and a profound comprehension of market elements. A few systems have demonstrated powerful in driving disturbance:

Innovation Development: Utilizing arising advancements to make novel items or administrations is a strong methodology. Innovations like man-made brainpower, blockchain, and the Web of Things can possibly reshape ventures.

Plan of action Development: Reconsidering customary plans of action by presenting membership administrations, pay-more only as costs arise estimating, or commercial center stages can upset laid out business sectors. Airbnb, for instance, reformed the housing business by empowering mortgage holders to lease their spaces.

Client Driven Plan: Putting the client at the focal point of item or administration improvement can prompt arrangements that address genuine trouble spots and convey a predominant client experience. Organizations like Apple have succeeded in this methodology.

Deft and Lean Standards: Spry turn of events and lean startup strategies underscore quick emphasis, client criticism, and consistent improvement. These standards permit disruptors to rapidly adjust to changing economic situations.

Associations and Biological systems: Working together with different organizations, framing organizations, or making environments can enhance the effect of interruption. For example, Tesla collaborated with different organizations to assemble charging foundation for electric vehicles.

Thrifty Advancement: Creating savvy arrangements that convey worth to clients in asset compelled conditions is a problematic methodology. Organizations like Xiaomi have embraced this technique in the purchaser gadgets market.

Market Passage and Extension: Entering new geographic business sectors or focusing on underserved client fragments can be a troublesome methodology. This frequently includes adjusting items or administrations to meet explicit territorial requirements.

Challenges in Disturbing Ventures

While upsetting enterprises can be fulfilling, it isn't without its portion of difficulties:

Obstruction from Officeholders: Laid out players in the business might oppose disturbance and utilize different strategies to keep up with their market predominance. This can incorporate campaigning for guidelines that favor officeholders or sending off counterattacks.

Administrative and Lawful Obstacles: Numerous ventures are dependent upon complex guidelines and legitimate systems. Exploring these administrative difficulties can be tedious and exorbitant for disruptors.

Capital and Assets: Problematic endeavors frequently require critical interest in examination, advancement, and promoting. Getting the vital capital and assets can be testing, particularly for new businesses.

Doubt and Reception Obstructions: Persuading clients to embrace new, problematic arrangements can be troublesome. Defeating suspicion and tending to reception obstructions is a vital test in disturbance.

Market Immersion: In mature business sectors, existing arrangements might have proactively soaked the market. Finding a traction for troublesome contributions can be an impressive errand.

Ability and Mastery: Drawing in and holding top ability with the abilities and skill expected to drive disturbance is a test. Profoundly talented experts are many times popular.

Financial Vulnerability: Monetary slumps or downturns can upset the plans and prospects of disruptors, influencing their admittance to capital and shopper spending.

Contextual analyses in Industry Disturbance

A few organizations have effectively upset enterprises by presenting creative items, administrations, and plans of action:

Uber: Uber changed the transportation business by presenting a ridesharing stage that interfaces drivers and travelers through a versatile application. The organization disturbed customary taxi administrations by offering an additional helpful and financially savvy elective.

Netflix: Netflix disturbed media outlets by changing from a DVD rental support of a streaming stage. It changed how individuals consume content, prompting a decrease in conventional satellite television memberships.

Airbnb: Airbnb upset the housing and accommodation industry by empowering property holders to lease their properties to voyagers. This imaginative methodology gave explorers extraordinary and financially savvy facilities while testing conventional lodgings.

Amazon: Amazon's internet business stage upset the retail business by offering an immense determination of items, helpful conveyance choices, and cutthroat costs. It changed how purchasers shop and reshaped the retail scene.

Tesla: Tesla disturbed the auto business by delivering top notch electric vehicles with state of the art innovation. Its attention on maintainability and development sped up the shift towards electric vehicles.

Alibaba: Alibaba reformed online business in China by interfacing organizations with a huge web-based buyer base. Its advanced installment stage, Alipay, has likewise disturbed conventional installment techniques.

The Job of Advanced Change in Industry Disturbance

Computerized change is a main thrust behind industry interruption. It includes the joining of advanced innovations into different parts of business activities, from client cooperations to inventory network the board. Key parts of advanced change in industry disturbance include:

Information Driven Direction: Outfitting the force of information and examination permits organizations to go with informed choices, recognize drifts, and foresee client conduct, which is urgent in disturbance.

Client Driven Concentration: Advanced change empowers organizations to assemble and investigate client information, improving the capacity to convey customized encounters and address client needs.

Process Improvement: Computerizing and streamlining cycles can prompt expense decreases and expanded productivity, which are indispensable for new companies and disruptors.

Development and Trial and error: Computerized change cultivates a culture of advancement and trial and error, empowering organizations to investigate novel thoughts and approaches constantly.

Light-footed Improvement: Nimble techniques are vital to advanced change, underlining quick cycle, versatility, and responsiveness to changing economic situations.

Network and Environments: Advanced change can work with the production of biological systems where different organizations team up and share information to convey more noteworthy worth to clients.

The Significance of Client Centricity in Industry Disturbance

A client driven approach is principal in industry disturbance. Putting the client at the focal point of item or administration improvement guarantees that contributions address genuine necessities and give a prevalent client experience. Key parts of a client driven approach include:

Understanding Client Needs: inside and out comprehension of client problem areas and inclinations is fundamental for planning troublesome arrangements that reverberate with the interest group.

Client Driven Plan: Client experience (UX) plan standards ought to direct item or administration improvement to make natural, easy to use interfaces that meet client assumptions.

Criticism Circles: Laying out criticism systems and effectively looking for client input empowers organizations to consistently further develop their contributions in view of certifiable utilization.

Personalization: Customized encounters and item suggestions can increment client commitment and devotion, separating troublesome arrangements from contenders.

Chapter 7

The Role of Mentorship

Mentorship is an idea as old as human development itself, yet its importance stays undiminished through the ages. In a world continually developing, mentorship is an evergreen practice that guides people along their excursion of individual and expert turn of events. The job of mentorship is diverse, incorporating an expansive range of perspectives going from professional success to self-improvement. This exposition investigates the profundity and expansiveness of mentorship, digging into its different structures and the persevering through influence it has on people, associations, and society.

Mentorship, at its center, is a relationship established on the trading of information, experience, and shrewdness between an accomplished individual, known as the tutor, and a less experienced one, known as the mentee. This trade isn't restricted to the exchange of genuine data however reaches out to the sharing of bits of knowledge, values, and viewpoints. The coach goes about as an aide, a sounding board, and a wellspring of motivation, while the mentee looks for information, counsel, and backing on their excursion of development.

In the domain of self-awareness, mentorship assumes a critical part. A coach can assist an individual with exploring the complicated maze of life, offering direction in navigation, critical thinking, and self-disclosure. The tutor fills in as a mirror, mirroring the mentee's assets and shortcomings, empowering mindfulness and self-awareness. This type of mentorship, frequently casual, happens inside families, companionships, or cozy connections, where people support each other in their quest for turning out to be better variants of themselves.

In an expert setting, mentorship is broadly perceived as an impetus for profession development and achievement. Numerous fruitful experts owe their achievements, to some extent to some extent, to the direction of coaches who shared their insight and ability. Guides help their protégés in figuring out the complexities of their picked field, putting forth objectives, and fostering the abilities important to succeed.

Also, mentorship frequently acquaints the mentee with important organizations and associations, further upgrading their vocation possibilities.

One of the amazing parts of mentorship is its flexibility to different fields and ventures. For example, in the realm of the scholarly world, mentorship is fundamental for supporting the up and coming age of researchers and analysts. Prepared teachers give significant direction to graduate understudies, showing them the complexities of exploration, distributing, and scholarly systems administration. In the business world, mentorship is similarly basic. Prepared business people and chiefs guide arising business pioneers, conferring industry information as well as the delicate abilities essential for progress, like administration, correspondence, and the capacity to appreciate individuals on a deeper level.

Mentorship likewise assumes a crucial part in encouraging development. In the tech business, for instance, coaches have frequently been instrumental in molding the professions of youthful trailblazers. Coaches share their experiences into arising innovations, support innovativeness, and proposition a place of refuge for trial and error. This guide mentee relationship frequently brings about historic revelations and problematic innovations that rethink ventures.

The guide mentee relationship is certainly not a road that goes only one direction. Coaches, in directing others, additionally experience individual and expert development. The method involved with educating and directing someone else can develop their comprehension own might interpret their field and upgrade their correspondence and initiative abilities. It is a harmonious relationship where the two players advantage, and this equal trade of information and experience is a demonstration of the persevering through nature of mentorship.

While mentorship has existed for quite a long time, its elements have developed to address the issues of contemporary society. In the cutting edge world, mentorship can be formal or casual, one-on-one or gathering based, face to face or virtual. Virtual mentorship, worked with by innovation, has become progressively predominant, permitting people to interface with guides and mentees from around the world, rising above geological limits.

The coming of the web and virtual entertainment has made it more straightforward for individuals to look for mentorship past their nearby circles. Online people group, discussions, and mentorship stages give a space to people to associate with tutors who can offer direction and backing in different spaces. This virtual mentorship model has democratized admittance to mentorship, making it feasible for people to associate with specialists in their picked fields no matter what their area.

In the working environment, formal mentorship programs have acquired notoriety as associations perceive the colossal advantages of sustaining ability from the inside. These projects are intended to coordinate workers with experienced coaches who can assist them with progressing in their vocations. Formal mentorship programs have shown to be a powerful method for holding ability, upgrade work fulfillment, and advance variety and incorporation inside associations.

Variety and incorporation are regions where mentorship can be especially effective. By matching underrepresented bunches with coaches who have effectively explored comparative difficulties, associations can establish a more comprehensive climate and engage people to get through hindrances. Coaches give direction, advocate for their mentees, and assist them with fostering the abilities and certainty expected to succeed in their vocations.

Mentorship projects can likewise be instrumental in authority advancement. Arising pioneers benefit from the direction of experienced coaches who can assist them with exploring the intricacies of positions of authority. Mentorship gives open doors to pioneers to consider their own initiative styles and ways of thinking, and it cultivates a culture of nonstop learning and improvement inside associations.

In instructive settings, mentorship takes on an exceptional job. Instructors and teachers act as coaches to understudies, directing them through the educational experience. This mentorship isn't restricted to scholastics yet stretches out to the advancement of decisive reasoning, critical thinking, and fundamental abilities. Viable instructing frequently includes components of mentorship, as teachers move understudies to investigate their interests, put forth objectives, and outline their ways to progress.

Mentorship isn't restricted to the expert or instructive domains; it reaches out into the individual existences of people also. In our current reality where the speed of life can be overpowering, individuals frequently look for guides to assist them with tracking down equilibrium, reason, and satisfaction. Life mentors and otherworldly aides act as coaches who give comprehensive direction and backing chasing individual satisfaction and prosperity.

Mentorship isn't just about making progress yet in addition about beating difficulty. In the midst of difficulty or emergency, people frequently go to tutors for basic reassurance and direction. A tutor can give a feeling of dependability and trust, offering shrewdness and viewpoint that helps the mentee explore troublesome conditions.

One of the amazing parts of mentorship is that it isn't restricted by age or experience. While it is normal for more seasoned and more experienced people to act as guides, mentorship can likewise be shared. More youthful people can guide their companions in regions where they have skill, and this friend mentorship can be similarly essentially as significant as additional conventional structures.

Notwithstanding one-on-one mentorship, bunch mentorship has built up some decent forward movement lately. Bunch mentorship includes a solitary coach directing a gathering of mentees. This organization considers divided growth opportunities and cultivates a feeling of local area between mentees. Bunch mentorship can be particularly helpful in tending to normal difficulties or objectives inside a local area or association.

The force of mentorship isn't just clear on a singular level yet additionally reaches out to whole networks and social orders. In burdened networks, mentorship programs can possibly break the pattern of destitution and disparity. By matching youngsters with coaches who can give direction and assets, these projects engage people to seek after training, profession open doors, and self-awareness.

Mentorship likewise assumes a huge part in the strengthening of ladies and minority gatherings. By and large, these gatherings have confronted fundamental boundaries and separation. Mentorship can assist with making everything fair by offering help and direction to people confronting one of a kind difficulties. Female guides, for instance, can rouse and enable different ladies to seek after influential positions and break unreasonable impediments.

7.1. The importance of guidance and support

Direction and backing are essential human necessities that rise above social, social, and financial limits. They are fundamental parts of self-awareness, training, and expert development. In a world set apart by intricacy and vulnerability, the meaning of direction and support couldn't possibly be more significant. This article investigates the multi-layered job of direction and backing in different parts of life, from schooling and professional success to individual prosperity and cultural advancement.

With regards to self-awareness, direction and backing are basic for people, all things considered. From youth to adulthood, individuals depend on direction and support to explore the difficulties and changes that life presents. Guardians, parental figures, educators, and tutors assume significant parts in giving direction and everyday encouragement, assisting people with building an underpinning of confidence, versatility, and a feeling of direction.

For youngsters, parental direction and backing are the foundations of sound turn of events. Guardians give the fundamental necessities of life as well as proposition close to home security and mentorship. They guide youngsters through their early stages, granting values, ingraining discipline, and sustaining their scholarly and profound development. This familial help establishes the groundwork for kids to become dependable, compassionate, and balanced grown-ups.

As kids progress through the school system, instructors and teachers assume the job of giving direction and backing. Instructors assist understudies with obtaining information, foster decisive reasoning abilities, and encourage an affection for learning. Past scholastics, instructors additionally act as coaches, offering counsel and support to assist understudies with defeating scholarly and individual difficulties.

In advanced education, scholastic counselors assume a significant part in directing understudies through their school or college experience. They assist understudies with picking courses, explore scholarly prerequisites, and plan for their future professions. This direction is important in guaranteeing that understudies pursue informed choices and progress toward their instructive objectives.

The significance of direction and backing reaches out to the domain of profession advancement. As people change from schooling to the labor force, they frequently look for the mentorship of experienced experts who can give bits of knowledge into their picked fields. Tutors offer exhortation on profession arranging, expertise advancement, and systems administration. They act as good examples, helping mentees put forth objectives and offering direction on the best way to accomplish them.

In the work environment, direction and backing are fundamental for proficient development and achievement. Administrators and managers give authority and mentorship to their groups, directing workers toward accomplishing hierarchical objectives. They offer input, set assumptions, and set out open doors for ability advancement. A strong workplace encourages worker resolve and efficiency, bringing about higher work fulfillment and maintenance.

Proficient associations and industry affiliations likewise offer direction and backing to their individuals. They give admittance to assets, preparing, and organizing amazing open doors that can assist people with progressing in their professions. These associations frequently offer mentorship programs that pair experienced experts with those looking for direction and backing.

Direction and backing are especially significant for people confronting vocation changes or difficulties. During seasons of employment cutback or vocation changes, people frequently look for the help of profession instructors or mentors. These experts assist people with surveying their abilities and interests, distinguish profession amazing open doors, and foster methodologies for accomplishing their vocation objectives. Their direction can be a help for those exploring unsure business circumstances.

In business and business, direction and backing are vital for startup achievement. Business visionaries frequently depend on tutors and guides who can give industry-explicit bits of knowledge, assist with refining business techniques, and interface them to likely financial backers or accomplices. The direction of experienced business visionaries can have the effect between a startup's prosperity and disappointment.

Direction and backing are not restricted to individual and expert turn of events; they likewise assume a critical part in mental and profound prosperity. In the present speedy and stress-filled world, numerous people wrestle with issues like tension, wretchedness, and other emotional well-being difficulties. Psychological well-being experts, like advisors, advocates, and specialists, offer direction and backing to assist people with adapting to these difficulties.

Specialists work with people to address a great many issues, from relationship issues and despondency to injury and dependence. They give a protected and secret space for clients to investigate their considerations and feelings, foster ways of dealing with especially difficult times, and work toward good change. The direction and backing given by psychological well-being experts can be life-putting something aside for those in emergency.

Notwithstanding formal emotional well-being experts, social emotionally support-ive networks, including loved ones, are fundamental for keeping up with mental and close to home prosperity. The presence of a solid emotionally supportive network can give a cushion against life's difficulties, lessening the gamble of psychological well-being issues and advancing versatility. Social help is especially vital during troublesome life changes, like separation, loss of a friend or family member, or a significant life altering event.

With regards to schooling, direction and backing are additionally essential for understudies with unique requirements. Specialized curriculum instructors and care staff work with understudies who have inabilities, assisting them with getting to the educational program and foster the abilities required for autonomy. These experts give customized direction and backing, guaranteeing that understudies get comprehensive and evenhanded schooling.

Besides, direction and backing are instrumental in encouraging variety and con-sideration. In an undeniably multicultural and interconnected world, people from assorted foundations face novel difficulties and open doors. Businesses, instructive establishments, and local area associations should give direction and support to guar-antee that individuals from all foundations have equivalent admittance to open doors and assets.

Direction and backing are especially significant for minimized and underrepre-sented gatherings, like ladies, racial and ethnic minorities, and the LGBTQ+ people group. Coaches and promoters inside these networks can offer direction and back-ing to assist people with conquering boundaries and accomplish their objectives. By tending to predisposition, segregation, and foundational imbalances, these guides and backers assume a basic part in propelling civil rights and consideration.

Cultural advancement additionally relies upon direction and emotionally support-ive networks. State run administrations and local area associations work to offer social types of assistance that help people and families out of luck. These administrations might incorporate lodging help,

food support, childcare projects, and admittance to medical services. By offering these assets, social orders expect to diminish disparity and give a security net to those confronting financial difficulties.

Direction and backing are especially indispensable for youngsters as they progress into adulthood. Youth coaching programs offer direction and good examples for in danger youth, assisting them with staying away from negative ways of behaving and settle on certain important decisions. These projects have been displayed to funda-mentally affect decreasing adolescent misconduct, working on instructive results, and advancing self-improvement.

Mentorship and direction are likewise significant with regards to local area im-provement and initiative. Local area pioneers, activists, and coordinators give direction and backing to people and gatherings trying to have a constructive outcome on their networks. By sharing their aptitude and upholding for social change, these pioneers move and activate others to pursue shared objectives.

One of the critical standards of powerful direction and backing is the idea of strengthening. Strengthening includes furnishing people with the information, abilities, and assets they need to pursue informed choices and assume command over their own lives. Strengthening is a center part of numerous direction and backing programs, whether in schooling, medical care, or local area improvement.

Strengthening is especially significant with regards to medical services. Patients benefit from medical services suppliers who analyze and regard ailments as well as engage them to come to informed conclusions about their wellbeing. Shared decision-production between medical care suppliers and patients is a developing pattern that perceives the significance of patient independence and informed decisions.

The strengthening of ladies has been a focal topic in conversations about orientation correspondence and ladies' freedoms. Ladies' strengthening includes advancing orientation value as well as furnishing ladies with the devices and assets they need to control their own lives and partake completely in the public eye. Projects and drives that help ladies' strengthening address many issues, from financial open doors and training to regenerative wellbeing and political cooperation.

7.2. The impact of experienced entrepreneurs

Experienced business visionaries are the foundation of advancement, financial development, and occupation creation in social orders all over the planet. They assume a basic part in molding ventures, driving mechanical progressions, and encouraging a culture of business. Their aggregate effect reaches out a long ways past their singular organizations, impacting the business environment, work potential open doors, and the generally financial scene. This paper investigates the complex effect of experienced business visionaries, from their commitments to work creation and financial development to their impact on startup culture and cultural turn of events.

One of the most immediate and substantial effects of experienced business people is work creation. New companies and private ventures, frequently established and drove by business visionaries, are liable for a huge piece of new position open doors in numerous economies. These endeavors enlist representatives as well as deal development potential and different profession ways.

Experienced business visionaries are knowledgeable in the specialty of occupation creation. They comprehend the significance of building compelling groups and distinguishing ability that can drive their organizations forward. As their endeavors grow and succeed, they recruit extra representatives, animating neighborhood and public economies by lessening joblessness rates and adding to generally speaking financial prosperity.

Notwithstanding sheer work numbers, experienced business people likewise encourage a culture of development that can prompt the formation of superior grade, well-paying position. They are frequently at the front line of embracing state of the art advancements and executing savvy fixes to address market needs. Thusly, they set out open doors for talented specialists in regions like programming improvement, information examination, computerized promoting, and high level assembling.

The effect of experienced business visionaries isn't restricted to coordinate work creation. Their impact swells through the whole business environment, moving others to seek after innovative undertakings. As fruitful business visionaries share their accounts, experiences, and mastery, they propel hopeful business pioneers and new companies, sustaining a pattern of development and business.

Experienced business people act as good examples, exhibiting that with devotion, flexibility, and the right technique, making business progress is conceivable. Their impact empowers a different exhibit of people to dive in and begin their own organizations, adding to the energy and dynamism of nearby and public economies.

Also, experienced business visionaries frequently take part in mentorship and holy messenger contributing, further supporting the startup environment. They give direction, support, and monetary assets to beginning phase business people, assisting them with exploring the difficulties of business. This mentorship and venture speeds up the development of new organizations as well as adds to a culture of information sharing and coordinated effort.

Experienced business people likewise assume a fundamental part in supporting development. Development is a critical driver of monetary development, and business visionaries are frequently at the bleeding edge of growing new items, administrations, and plans of action. These developments can possibly change whole businesses and work on the personal satisfaction for society at large.

Experienced business people comprehend the significance of remaining on the ball in a quickly developing business scene. They are bound to put resources into innovative work, cultivating the formation of weighty advancements and arrangements. Whether it's a startup fostering a progressive application or a laid out business person driving an assembling development, these commitments have sweeping impacts available and customers.

Besides, experienced business people are knowledgeable in perceiving arising patterns and market holes. They rush to distinguish open doors for advancement and development, utilizing their industry information to foster arrangements that meet advancing buyer needs. This capacity to expect and adjust to change is a main impetus in financial advancement.

Business people additionally add to financial development through their part in global exchange and venture. As organizations extend, they frequently look for potential chances to enter new business sectors or lay out worldwide stock chains. This development adds to expanded commodities, imports, and unfamiliar direct speculation, encouraging financial relationship and worldwide development.

Experienced business visionaries, who have a profound comprehension of the complexities of global business, are strategically set up to drive trade situated procedures.

They not just make items and administrations for the worldwide market yet in addition grow their organizations by cooperating with unfamiliar partners and taking part in global exchange missions and arrangements. This worldwide standpoint advances financial participation and shared development among countries.

The effect of experienced business visionaries on financial development isn't restricted to the homegrown market. They likewise affect the allure of their nations of origin to unfamiliar financial backers. At the point when experienced business visionaries make fruitful organizations, they act as verification of a good business climate, empowering unfamiliar organizations and financial backers to think about entering the market.

Experienced business visionaries can likewise add to financial development through consolidations and acquisitions (M&A) exercises. As their organizations develop, they might try to procure or converge with different organizations to grow their market reach or upgrade their abilities. These M&A exercises drive development as well as lead to the solidification of industry players, which can animate further advancement and rivalry.

Notwithstanding their effect on the business and financial scene, experienced business visionaries likewise significantly affect cultural turn of events. They frequently take part in magnanimous exercises and local area association, rewarding the networks that have upheld their organizations. These commitments incorporate a large number of drives, from instructive help to ecological maintainability.

Instruction is a typical focal point of magnanimity for experienced business visionaries. They comprehend the significance of training in outfitting people with the abilities and information they need to prevail in the cutting edge labor force. Subsequently, they frequently lay out instructive establishments or backing existing projects, which can prompt better admittance to quality schooling for underserved populaces.

Moreover, experienced business people can assume an essential part in tending to cultural difficulties through their generous endeavors. Numerous business people are profoundly dedicated to resolving issues like destitution, medical care abberations, and natural maintainability. Their commitments to social causes can have a significant effect, whether by supporting medical care drives, putting resources into clean energy arrangements, or upholding for civil rights.

Experienced business visionaries are much of the time engaged with molding public strategy and pushing for business-accommodating guidelines. They influence their business intuition and industry information to impact government choices that influence their endeavors as well as the more extensive business local area. Their promotion can prompt approaches that encourage business venture, development, and financial development.

This promotion incorporates partaking in open confidential organizations, adding to industry affiliations, and participating in campaigning endeavors. Experienced business people utilize their foundation to guarantee that the interests of the business local area are addressed in government choices. Thusly, they assist with establishing a climate helpful for business and business extension.

As far as cultural turn of events, experienced business visionaries can likewise show others how its done with regards to moral strategic approaches and corporate social obligation (CSR). They perceive the significance of working organizations in a moral and reasonable way, not just in light of the fact that it is the proper thing to do yet in addition since it can decidedly affect their primary concern and notoriety.

CSR drives started by experienced business visionaries can include a scope of exercises, from executing economical inventory network practices and lessening fossil fuel byproducts to advancing fair work practices and local area commitment. By focusing on friendly and natural obligation, they set norms for different organizations to follow, empowering more extensive cultural change.

Experienced business people additionally add to the advancement of social capital, which is vital for building trust, participation, and solid networks. They frequently assume dynamic parts in nearby and public organizations, uniting people, organizations, and associations to address normal difficulties and open doors.

These business visionaries have a broad organization of contacts and connections, and they are strategically set up to interface partners, share information, and encourage coordinated effort. Their capacity to connect holes and work with organizations adds to the development and dependability of networks and ventures.

The effect of experienced business people is additionally apparent in their commitment with arising advances and development. They comprehend that remaining serious in the computerized age requires a readiness to embrace and put resources into groundbreaking innovations. As early adopters and financial backers in tech-driven arrangements, they add to the advanced change of enterprises.

7.3. Navigating the entrepreneurial ecosystem

The enterprising biological system is a dynamic and complex climate that envelops a huge number of interconnected components, from new companies and financial backers to help associations and government strategies. Exploring this environment is a difficult however fundamental undertaking for hopeful business people and business pioneers. This paper investigates the diverse enterprising biological system, digging into the key parts that make up this complex scene and talking about the techniques and assets fundamental for effectively navigating it.

Grasping the Pioneering Environment

The enterprising environment is an expansive and comprehensive idea that incorporates every one of the variables and entertainers that impact business venture inside a given locale or industry. It is portrayed by its dynamism, as it persistently advances because of financial, innovative, and social changes. This environment involves a few interrelated parts:

1. **Business people:** At the center of the biological system are the business people themselves, people who consider, make, and oversee organizations. They come from assorted foundations, and their advancements drive monetary development, make occupations, and encourage advancement.

2. **New companies:** These are recently settled organizations, frequently in the beginning phases of advancement. New businesses assume a pivotal part in the biological system, as they are a critical wellspring of development and financial development. They are described by their spryness, risk-taking, and problematic potential.

3. **Financial backers:** Financial backers, like financial speculators, private backers, and confidential value firms, give the monetary assets that new companies need to develop and scale. Their capital infusion is indispensable for transforming imaginative thoughts into practical organizations.

4. **Support Associations:** These incorporate hatcheries, gas pedals, and collaborating spaces that offer assets, mentorship, and systems administration valuable open doors for business people. They assume an imperative part in assisting new businesses with exploring the difficulties of beginning phase development.

5. **Colleges and Exploration Foundations:** Scholarly establishments add to the environment by cultivating development, leading examination, and teaching the up and coming age of business people. They are center points of information and ability that frequently team up with new companies and industry.

6. **Enterprises:** Enormous organizations are contenders as well as likely accomplices for new businesses. They can offer assets, circulation channels, and open doors for coordinated effort. Partnerships hoping to enhance might gain new businesses or structure key unions.

7. **Government Arrangements:** Government strategies, including charge motivating forces, guidelines, and subsidizing programs, shape the enterprising climate. Strategies that advance business can fundamentally affect the biological system's wellbeing and dynamic quality.

8. **Encouraging groups of people:** Casual organizations, industry affiliations, and expert gatherings assume a part in associating business visionaries, sharing information, and cultivating a feeling of local area among similar people.

9. **Clients and Markets:** The interest for inventive items and administrations drives pioneering exercises. Understanding client needs and market elements is fundamental for new businesses to succeed.

Exploring the Environment: Systems and Assets

Exploring the enterprising biological system can be testing, given its intricacy and intensity. Notwithstanding, business visionaries can take on procedures and influence assets to assist them with prevailing in this unique climate.

1. **Building Areas of strength for a:** Systems administration is a principal part of business venture. Creating associations with different business visionaries, tutors, financial backers, and industry experts can give significant experiences, direction, and valuable open doors. Building areas of strength for a can open ways to financing, organizations, and business improvement.

2. **Recognizing the Perfect Times:** Effective business people have a sharp capacity to distinguish market valuable open doors and neglected needs. Directing statistical surveying, remaining refreshed on industry drifts, and being receptive to client criticism are fundamental for perceiving where development can happen.

3. **Getting to Subsidizing:** Financing is in many cases a basic calculate transforming a startup thought into a suitable business. Business visionaries can investigate different sources of financial support, including bootstrapping, heavenly messenger speculation, funding, crowdfunding, and government awards. It's essential to coordinate the money source with the particular necessities and phase of the business.

4. **Looking for Help from Hatcheries and Gas pedals:** Hatcheries and gas pedals give new companies significant assets, mentorship, and admittance to networks. These projects can assist business visionaries with refining their plans of action, access subsidizing, and speed up their development.

5. **Embracing Advancement:** Business is innately connected to development. Business visionaries ought to ceaselessly look for better approaches to work on their items, administrations, and cycles. Remaining imaginative is a vital figure keeping an upper hand on the lookout.

6. **Adjusting to Market Changes:** The business scene is dynamic, and new companies should be versatile. Having the option to turn and change procedures in light of changing economic situations is a vital expertise for business people.

7. **Utilizing Innovation:** Innovation assumes a focal part in current business venture. Utilizing advanced devices, information investigation, and online stages can smooth out activities, upgrade client commitment, and arrive at more extensive business sectors.

8. **Figuring out Lawful and Administrative Structures:** Business people should explore legitimate and administrative systems that fluctuate by industry and area. Having a fundamental comprehension of licensed innovation, contract regulation, and significant guidelines is fundamental to safeguard financial matters and guarantee consistence.

9. **Overseeing Chance:** Business venture innately implies risk. Viable gamble the executives, which incorporates evaluating and moderating dangers, is fundamental for the drawn out progress of a startup. Understanding when and how to proceed with reasonable plans of action is an expertise that can fundamentally influence an endeavor's direction.

10. **Encouraging a Culture of Learning:** The enterprising excursion is a persistent growth opportunity. Business people ought to embrace a development outlook, be available to input, and gain from the two triumphs and disappointments.

11. **Adjusting Enthusiasm and Sober mindedness:** While energy and vision are main impetuses behind business, practicality and an emphasis on benefit are similarly significant. Finding some kind of harmony among enthusiasm and reasonableness is really difficult for business people.

12. **Drawing in with Clients:** Building areas of strength for a with clients is imperative. Business visionaries ought to effectively look for criticism, pay attention to client needs, and utilize this data to refine their items and administrations.

13. **Exploring Legitimate and Moral Difficulties:** Business visionaries should settle on moral choices and explore lawful difficulties. Understanding the moral ramifications of business choices and looking for lawful insight when required can forestall expensive errors.

14. **Conquering Disappointment:** Disappointment is a characteristic piece of business venture. Figuring out how to return from difficulties, adjust, and drive forward is a sign of fruitful business visionaries. Flexibility is a critical characteristic in exploring the biological system.

15. **Remaining Informed and Adjusting:** The pioneering scene is in consistent motion, with recent fads, advancements, and market elements arising routinely. Business visionaries should remain informed, adjust to change, and stay adaptable in their methodologies.

Government Strategies and Business

Government strategies assume a critical part in molding the enterprising biological system. Business venture well disposed arrangements can establish a climate helpful for business creation and development. These approaches might incorporate duty motivators, awards, subsidizing programs, and administrative structures that diminish obstructions to section for new companies. Besides, strategies that advance schooling and research foundations can add to a gifted labor force and encourage development.

****Admittance to Capital:** Taxpayer supported initiatives that give admittance to capital can be a huge asset for new companies. These may incorporate awards, credits, and value speculation programs intended to help business people in the beginning phases of business improvement.

Administrative Climate: A straightforward and unsurprising administrative climate is significant for business people. Administrative obstacles can be hindrances to section for new businesses. Legislatures that intend to cultivate business venture ought to smooth out processes and diminish administrative noise.

Protected innovation Security: Licensed innovation privileges are basic for safeguarding development. Government strategies that give solid licensed innovation security can give business people the certainty to put resources into innovative work.

7.4. Building a valuable network

In a world set apart by interconnectivity and worldwide correspondence, constructing a significant organization has turned into a fundamental expertise. Whether for self-improvement, professional success, or innovative achievement, a solid and various organization can open ways to new open doors, offer help, and encourage coordinated effort. This paper investigates the complexities of building a significant organization, examining the significance of systems administration, procedures for network improvement, and the persevering through advantages of a deep rooted network.

Understanding the Significance of Systems administration

Organizing isn't simply a social practice however an essential undertaking with significant ramifications for individual and expert turn of events. It includes the purposeful work to interface with others, share information, and assemble connections that can add to one's objectives and yearnings. The significance of systems administration can be figured out through a few key viewpoints:

1. **Admittance to Potential open doors:** A significant organization can give admittance to a great many open doors, from employment opportunities and business associations to mentorship and speculation. Potential open doors frequently move through special interactions, and a solid organization goes about as a course for these possibilities.

2. **Information and Skill:** Organizations are priceless wellsprings of information and aptitude. Through associations, people can take advantage of the aggregate insight of their organization, acquiring bits of knowledge, counsel, and admittance to data that may not be promptly accessible somewhere else.

3. **Backing and Direction:** An organization offers an emotionally supportive network that can be especially valuable during testing times. Whether confronting individual or expert hindrances, people can go to their organization for counsel, consolation, and help.

4. **Coordinated effort and Organizations:** Systems administration cultivates cooperation and associations. By associating with similar people, experts can find likely teammates, fellow benefactors, or accomplices who share their vision and can assist with carrying their plans to completion.

5. **Self-awareness:** Communicating with different people in an organization can widen one's point of view and invigorate self-awareness. Openness to novel thoughts, societies, and encounters can enhance one's life and viewpoint.

6. **Professional success:** Systems administration is a vital driver of professional success. It can prompt work references, advancements, and admittance to powerful chiefs. In numerous ventures, connections worked through systems administration are an essential consider profession achievement.

Techniques for Building a Significant Organization

Building a significant organization requires an intentional and insightful methodology. It includes supporting connections, offering worth to other people, and persistently growing one's circle of associations. Here are a few methodologies for compelling organization improvement:

1. **Characterize Your Goals:** The most vital phase in building an important organization is to explain your targets. What do you expect to accomplish through systems administration? Whether it's getting another line of work, acquiring industry bits of knowledge, or laying out a steady local area, defining clear objectives will direct your endeavors.

2. **Recognize Key Contacts:** Distinguish people who are decisively situated to assist you with accomplishing your objectives. These key contacts might be guides, industry specialists, possible businesses, or individual business people. Zeroing in on these associations permits you to really assign your time and exertion.

3. **Go to Systems administration Occasions:** Systems administration occasions, like meetings, classes, studios, and industry get-togethers, give incredible chances to meet new individuals and trade thoughts. Try to go to occasions applicable to your objectives and interests.

4. **Influence Online Entertainment:** In the computerized age, virtual entertainment stages offer amazing assets for systems administration. Stages like LinkedIn, Twitter, and Facebook permit you to associate with experts, take part in industry conversations, and grandstand your ability.

5. **Offer Worth:** Powerful systems administration isn't exclusively about what you can acquire yet in addition about what you can offer. Give assistance, counsel, or backing to your organization contacts. By offering worth to other people, you lay out a standing as a significant association.

6. **Follow Up:** In the wake of meeting somebody in your organization, it's vital to follow up and keep up with the association. Send a thank-you email, interface via online entertainment, or timetable a subsequent gathering to keep the relationship dynamic.

7. **Differentiate Your Organization:** A significant organization is an assorted organization. Incorporate people from various foundations, ventures, and socioeconomics. Variety enhances your viewpoint as well as expands your possible open doors.

8. **Construct Certifiable Connections:** Genuineness is a critical calculate building enduring connections. Be earnest in your collaborations, take a certified revenue in others, and develop connections in view of trust and shared regard.

9. **Be Steady:** Building a significant organization is a continuous interaction. Consistency in your endeavors is fundamental. Routinely check in with your organization contacts, offer help, and remain refreshed on their exercises and needs.

10. **Join Proficient Associations:** Many fields have proficient associations and affiliations that offer open doors for systems administration. Think about turning into an individual from these associations to get to an organization of companions and industry specialists.

11. **Take part in Humanitarian effort:** Chipping in for purposes you are energetic about benefits the local area as well as acquaints you with similar people who share your qualities. It's a significant method for extending your organization while having a constructive outcome.

12. **Show restraint:** Building an important organization takes time. Connections need supporting and may not yield prompt outcomes. Be patient and steady in your systems administration endeavors.

The Getting through Advantages of a Deep rooted Organization

A deeply grounded network is a priceless resource with getting through benefits that can impact different parts of your own and proficient life. The upsides of a solid organization include:

1. **Admittance to Valuable open doors:** Your organization fills in as a passage to various open doors. Whether you're looking for a new position, a business organization, or venture, your associations can give presentations and suggestions that fundamentally increment your odds of coming out on top.

2. **Proficient Turn of events:** Through your organization, you approach coaches and specialists who can offer direction and mentorship. Gaining from those with more experience can speed up your expert turn of events and give important bits of knowledge.

3. **Industry Bits of knowledge:** Systems administration opens you to the most recent industry patterns, experiences, and advancements. Remaining informed about your field's improvements can assist you with pursuing informed choices and adjust to changes in your industry.

4. **Emotionally supportive network:** in the midst of challenge or difficulty, your organization fills in as an emotionally supportive network. Whether you're confronting a lifelong difficulty, individual emergency, or an extreme business choice, the support and direction of your organization can be significant.

5. **Cooperative Open doors:** A deep rooted network is prolific ground for cooperative open doors. You might find likely accomplices, prime supporters, or teammates who share your vision and can assist with carrying your activities and thoughts to completion.

6. **Self-improvement:** Interfacing with a different and proficient organization can invigorate self-improvement and expand your perspectives. Openness to alternate points of view, encounters, and societies can improve your life and develop how you might interpret the world.

7. **Professional success:** Systems administration is a vital driver of professional success. It can prompt work references, advancements, and admittance to persuasive chiefs. Your organization can be the wellspring of new vocation open doors that may not be freely publicized.

8. **Notoriety Building:** A deep rooted organization can add to building a positive expert standing. Your contacts can vouch for your abilities, skill, and unwavering quality, improving your validity and reliability in your field.

9. **Various Viewpoints:** A different organization opens you to a large number of points of view and perspectives. This variety can challenge your suspicions, invigorate inventiveness, and give a balanced point of view on different issues and difficulties.

10. **Individual and Expert Satisfaction:** At last, a deeply grounded network adds to individual and expert satisfaction. The connections you fabricate can improve your life, giving a feeling of having a place, achievement, and importance.

www.ingramcontent.com/pod-product-compliance
Lightning Source LLC
LaVergne TN
LVHW050634200726
843506LV00010B/1247